Government Contracts Negotiation, Simplified!

The Plain English Guide to Redlining Federal
Contracts and Subcontracts, FAR Clauses, and
Common Contract Sections

Christoph Mlinarchik
www.ChristophLLC.com
Christoph@ChristophLLC.com

About the Author, Christoph Mlinarchik

Christoph LLC delivers expert advice in government contracts: consulting, expert witness services, and professional training. Contact Christoph LLC for solutions or to receive free, monthly updates about government contracts: Christoph@ChristophLLC.com.

The owner Christoph Mlinarchik, JD, CFCM, PMP (Certified Federal Contract Manager, Project Management Professional) is an attorney, expert witness, professional instructor, consultant, frequent public speaker, nationally recognized subject matter expert, and award-winning author of 75+ publications on government contracts and acquisitions, including the books *Government Contracts in Plain English* (available at https://www.amazon.com/dp/173419815X/) and *Federal Acquisition Regulation (FAR) in Plain English* (https://www.amazon.com/dp/1734198117/) and *Government Contracts Negotiation, Simplified! The Plain English Guide to Redlining Federal Contracts and Subcontracts, FAR Clauses, and Common Contract Sections*. These books are part of *The Government Contracts in Plain English Series*: https://www.amazon.com/dp/B09MRCMWBD

Christoph was honored with the "Top Professionals Under 40" and "Best Article" awards by the National Contract Management Association (NCMA). Christoph Mlinarchik is an experienced expert witness who has delivered expert opinions and reports, research concerning damages, key findings, and valuable case strategy for complicated contract litigation.

Christoph's consulting clients include businesses that deal with information technology (IT), professional services, defense, cybersecurity, construction, medical and health care, intelligence, national security, research, science, technology, and several other sectors.

Christoph has taught or trained 1,000+ federal, military, and contractor professionals nationwide—from novices to C-level executives. Businesses and individuals rely on Christoph's expertise to navigate the complex federal contracting marketplace. Contracts managers, attorneys, chief executive officers, program managers, sales directors, business capture and proposal experts, and other contracting professionals consistently provide outstanding reviews for Christoph's consulting expertise, teaching skills, presentation style, and client satisfaction.

Christoph has negotiated, reviewed, or managed billions of dollars of government contracts over the course of his career. This real-world experience provides an invaluable perspective for clients.

Table of Contents

Section 1: Negotiation Fundamentals

Section 2: Negotiation Mechanics

Table of Contents, Continued

Section 3: Negotiation Perspectives

CHAPTER 1, INTRODUCTION

Negotiating government contracts and subcontracts can be complex and difficult, but this book makes it simple and easy for you. My third book summarizes the most common government contract clauses, explains the mechanics of contract negotiation, and delivers short, practical insights to guide your decisions. The last few chapters explore the negotiation strength and motivation of your potential partners, such as prime contractors, subcontractors, the government, or individual employees.

By reading my plain English explanations, you gain confidence in what your contract means, how you should negotiate, and what you can expect from your negotiation partners.

Absorb these insights I developed across years of experience in a variety of government contracting positions. I have been a federal contracting officer, Judge Advocate General acquisitions attorney, professional instructor, consultant to major corporations, small business policy advisor, and expert witness in multimillion-dollar contracting litigation. In each of these roles, negotiating and understanding contracts was crucial in my success. Learn my tips so that you can apply them in your own negotiations.

How can this book help me with government contract negotiation?

My third book simplifies the negotiation process, explains critical clauses, and demystifies the most important concepts.

Your confidence and competence will grow as you learn the meaning of important contract clauses, sections, and headings. Learn the fundamental concepts so you can avoid problems and make better business deals. Negotiating and "marking up" or *redlining* contracts is an essential business skill that can make or break your company, so reading my book is a starting point.

Finally, by learning the priorities and perspectives of different negotiation partners, such as the government, prime contractors, and subcontractors, you can gain the bargaining edge by understanding the other side. Learning more about your potential negotiation partners will help you to anticipate their needs, tactics, and strategies.

How is this book organized?

Each chapter stands on its own, but the first 10 chapters explore the fundamental concepts of the Federal Acquisition Regulation (FAR), which heavily affects both prime contractors and subcontractors. The second section delves into the mechanics of negotiation with practical advice. The third section explores the perspectives of the common negotiation partners like subcontractors, the government, or prime contractors. Finally, the very last chapter, "Common Contract Sections in Plain English," translates and demystifies critical contracting clauses.

What other books should I read to learn more about government contracts?

The fact that you are reading this book proves you are the target audience of my two earlier bestselling books, *Government Contracts in Plain English* (available at https://www.amazon.com/dp/173419815X) and *Federal Acquisition Regulation in Plain English* (available at https://www.amazon.com/dp/1734198117). The first book offers practical advice, lists pitfalls to avoid, and delivers insider insights that demystify the federal contracting industry. The second book answers 700+ frequently asked questions (FAQ) about the Federal Acquisition Regulation and provides a "highlight reel" of all 53 Parts of the FAR. Complete *The Government Contracts in Plain English Series*: https://www.amazon.com/dp/B09MRCMWBD

Do you assist companies with government contract and subcontract negotiation?

Yes! I started my company www.ChristophLLC.com years ago to offer expert advice on government contracting. My company delivers consulting advice to federal contractors and subcontractors, professional training, and expert witness services. Much of the work involves contract and subcontract negotiation, including *redlining* and suggesting changes, additions, and deletions. Feel free to send me an email: Christoph@ChristophLLC.com.

Do you help individual persons, not just companies?

Of course! My clients include individuals, employees, sole proprietors, and entrepreneurs—not just growing or mature companies. Christoph LLC can help you to negotiate a new job opportunity, to improve your resume, to achieve your long-term career goals, or to start a business.

Do you have experience negotiating on behalf of both the government and contractors?

Yes, I have negotiation experience in *both* the public and the private sector.

In my previous career as a federal employee, I negotiated contracts on behalf of the US government. You can learn some very important lessons when you negotiate against the largest and most powerful defense contractors, such as Boeing, Raytheon, and Lockheed Martin. I also designed solicitations, requests for proposals (RFP), requests for quotes (RFQ), statements of work (SOW), and I managed the competition, evaluation, selection, award, and administration of federal contracts. In sum, I composed and negotiated contracts for the largest client in the history of the world — the US government, which spends more than 1 trillion dollars each year.

In the private sector, I am a qualified expert witness in the field of government contracting. In addition to consulting for scores of companies through www.ChristophLLC.com, I previously worked as the director of policy and acquisitions (government contracting expert) for a defense contractor. I have also worked alongside the government client as an onsite contractor, serving as an advisor and subject matter expert (SME) in government contracting. Finally, I professionally teach the full range of government contracting subjects, including the negotiation of contracts and subcontracts. The benefit to you is that I distilled my skills, experience, and expertise into this book, all delivered in plain English for easy reading.

What is one reason clients hire Christoph LLC?

My clients love how I explain complicated things in a simple way. In fact, my streamlining is the primary reason why they hire me. They need an expert who can discover the important issues quickly and deliver plans of action that solve their problems. Don't you want someone to make it simple for you? I use as little jargon or confusing words as possible with my clients. I provide details when appropriate, but I always give the *bottom line up front* or *BLUF*. Whether I'm teaching a class of 50 students or advising the CEO of a corporation, I deliver real world, practical advice.

Is this book an expert witness report with precise and cautious statements?

No, this book is not an expert witness report.

Is this book legal advice? Is this book tax advice? Is this book accounting advice?

No, no, and no! This book is not legal advice, which should come from a licensed attorney. My book is not tax advice, which should come from a competent tax professional. This book is not accounting advice, which should come from a certified public accountant (CPA).

Will this book substitute for specific negotiation advice and assistance?

No! If you have a specific problem, you need a specific answer from a competent professional. My email address is Christoph@ChristophLLC.com.

Why is this book written in question-and-answer format?

This question-and-answer format is familiar to anyone who has read a *frequently asked questions* (FAQ) document. By writing my book in a question-and-answer format, you feel like we're having a conversation as you read it. Finally, reading questions and answers trains your mind to ask the right questions, and it accelerates your reading pace.

Can I hire you for consulting, training, expert witness services, or to help me with contract negotiation?

Maybe. Email me at Christoph@ChristophLLC.com. You can read more about my background and company at www.ChristophLLC.com.

Have you written any other government contracting books?

Yes! Check out my two bestselling earlier books, available in paperback and Kindle editions on Amazon. Buy all three to complete the trilogy!

Government Contracts in Plain English is available at:
https://www.amazon.com/dp/173419815X/

Federal Acquisition Regulation in Plain English is available at:
https://www.amazon.com/dp/1734198117

Buy all the books in *The Government Contracts in Plain English Series*: https://www.amazon.com/dp/B09MRCMWBD

CHAPTER 2, REDLINING CONTRACTS

How important are the incremental changes during the contract negotiation process?

If you reconsider your business lifecycle as a series of decisions in time, the snapshots of negotiation decisions always stand out. In just a day, a week, or a month — maybe in just a brief moment — your business negotiates terms that will ripple on for years or decades. Negotiation decisions can change your future income by millions of dollars or even billions. For this reason, you should carefully track the step-by-step process of negotiation by tracking all the changes using the process called *redlining*.

What is redlining?

Some people call the contract negotiation process *redlining* because you trade versions of the contract with all proposed changes tracked. You receive the first version of the contract. You *redline* the contract by making textual changes — adding, editing, or deleting text. You document your alterations by using the *track changes* feature in your word-processing software.

You send the material back. Your negotiation partner can see what you propose and accept or reject the changes identified by new *redlines*. Your negotiation partner returns the contract to you with any new redlines of his own that identify any other alterations. This process can go on indefinitely.

Why is this process called redlining?

The word-processing software (for example, Microsoft Word) displays the tracked changes using red text. The *track changes* function shows new or additional text in red lettering. Deleted text is identified by a red line stricken through the removed words or phrases, mimicking the earlier days of pen-and-ink changes. Over time, this process of changing the text — and recording these changes to be shown to your negotiation counterpart — became known as *redlining*. If your software displays these changes using some other color, blue perhaps, do not dwell on this difference. You are still *redlining* because the word has become a *term of art* in the contracting industry. Do not refer to "blue-lining" or some other term, which would confuse people.

Should you always use and demand redlining for contract negotiation?

Yes, always use redlining and keep track of all changes. Always demand that your negotiation partner use the redlining and change-tracking features.

What if my negotiation partner did not track the changes using redlining?

If your negotiation partner sends over a changed contractual document that does not display the proposed changes, you should politely request a version that includes the redlines. Train all your negotiation partners to follow this process. Be firm but respectful.

Your negotiation partner may be innocent or naïve, but sending a changed contractual document without the redlines to highlight those changes can be considered rude, lazy, or deceptive. Give everyone the benefit of the doubt for the first offense, but beware of anyone who repeatedly fails to show you all new redlining. Repeat offenders may have reason to hide the changes from you, which means the changes are probably not in your favor! Redlines were designed to prevent the possibility of any change that is surprising. Use redlining!

What are the benefits of using redlining for contract negotiation?

Redlining has two benefits. First, it lets you see exactly what your negotiation partner proposes or changes. Second, it documents the negotiation process thoroughly for any future negotiations. Over time, you can grasp the habits, desires, and motives of your frequent business partners. Maybe you can anticipate their next moves.

Should you include comments with your redlines?

Yes, add comments that explain your proposed changes. Most professionals include "comment balloons" in the margins of the pages. The "comment balloon" adds text that is not part of the contract itself, but which everyone can see. The final contract will not show any of these "comment balloons" or other redlines.

Every comment you write helps your negotiation partner understand your position and reasoning. Communication accelerates compromise, so offer detailed comments when appropriate. You can justify your policy, calculate your risk, provide specific examples, or explain your disagreements. Sharing comments can save unnecessary meetings and prevent misunderstandings.

Can you reply to your negotiation partner's comments?

Yes, you can reply directly to your negotiation partner's comments. The comments and replies will document the back-and-forth negotiations, so you can track your progress.

How should you label redlined contract files?

Keeping track of multiple versions of the same document can be confusing. To simplify the process, use file names that show date and version. For example, the file name "Christoph LLC consulting contract v.4 08.30.2035" designates the fourth version of a contract that was edited on August 30, 2035.

How should you label the final or "clean" contract file?

After negotiating the contract, create a copy of the final contract that accepts (or rejects) all changes and deletes all comments. This final version that shows no redlines is called a "clean" version. The "clean" version is helpful for review, but you should also save all of the redlined versions so you will know exactly what has changed from the original.

When should you strike or delete clauses in the contract?

Striking (deleting) clauses is a critical part of the negotiation process both for prime contractors and subcontractors. Your negotiation partner will try to force you to accept clauses that you should not accept. These unnecessary or inappropriate clauses may benefit your negotiation partner, or they may result from laziness or ignorance. No matter the reason, you need to protect your company. Do not be afraid to strike, delete, or modify clauses.

How can you tell which FAR clauses are appropriate for the contract?

Federal Acquisition Regulation (FAR) clauses contain their own instructions for when to include them in prime contracts or subcontracts. These instructions are called *prescription clauses*. Read more in the following chapter, "Prescription Clauses."

CHAPTER 3, PRESCRIPTION CLAUSES

What is a prescription clause?

Prescription clauses explain to the contracting officer whether or not to include specific FAR clauses within new government contracts. At the beginning of the full text of every FAR clause, there is a message to the contracting officer that explains when to insert the clause into government (prime) contracts. This message or instruction to the contracting officer is known as the *prescription clause*.

Prescription clauses are found in the FAR, because the FAR applies to the contracting officer who writes the government contract. (Read more about this topic in the chapter, "No, the FAR Does Not Apply to Government Contractors.")

Why is the prescription clause so important?

Your company will negotiate with the government as to which clauses truly belong in the contract. To win, appeal to the official instructions to the contracting officer in the FAR. These explicit instructions are called the *prescription clauses*.

Every FAR clause has a prescription clause that explains exactly when to use the FAR clause in government contracts. Therefore, knowing how to reference a prescription clause is naturally one of your most powerful negotiation tools.

How can you track down the prescription clause for a FAR clause?

Read the first sentence of the full text of the FAR clause, which is usually a reference to the prescription clause. Here's an example for FAR clause 52.243-1, Changes – Fixed-Price (Aug 1987). The first sentence you read below the title is a reference to the prescription clause:

> "As prescribed in [FAR] 43.205(a)(1), insert the following clause."

The prescription clause itself is FAR 43.205(a)(1). That reference is where you find the instruction to the contracting officer that explains when to insert the clause into the contract. The actual text of the prescription clause is found at FAR 43.205(a)(1):

> "The contracting officer shall insert the clause at [FAR] 52.243-1, Changes – Fixed-Price, in solicitations and contracts when a fixed-price contract for supplies is contemplated."

Now you know that this clause must be in government contracts for supplies that are fixed-price. You have the knowledge you need to negotiate a deletion of this clause in your government contract if it is inapplicable.

How can I convince the contracting officer to remove the FAR clause?

If your government contract is for services rather than supplies, you know now that FAR 52.243-1, Changes – Fixed-Price does not belong. The prescription clause explains that including the clause is incorrect. If the government includes this clause in your contract, you must request its removal. In your polite and respectful email message (or within the *redlining* in the document), you should specifically mention the prescription clause. You can write something like this:

> "We respectfully request removal of FAR 52.243-1, "Changes – Fixed-Price" from this contract. The prescription clause at FAR 43.205(a)(1) states that FAR 52.243-1 is appropriate for contracts for supplies. As this government contract is for services, and not for supplies, please remove FAR 52.243-1."

This way is the most persuasive method to negotiate the removal of a clause with a contracting officer. By appealing to the legitimate authority of the FAR itself, the contracting officer has no choice but to comply.

Are prescription clauses relevant to federal contractors in addition to contracting officers?

Note that this guidance—this specific *prescription clause*—applies to the government contracting officer, not to your company as the prime contractor. Within the FAR prescription clause, there is no language directing your company, the prime contractor, to include this clause in any subcontracts.

However, *within the clause itself* (rather than its prescription), there may be language that requires your company to include some version of the clause in subcontracts. This type of language, requiring prime contractors to include clauses in subcontracts, is called a *flow-down prescription clause.* Read more about *flow-down prescription clauses* in the next chapter, "Flow-Down Clauses."

CHAPTER 4, FLOW-DOWN CLAUSES

What is a flow-down clause?

Generally, a *flow-down clause* is any contract clause that a prime contractor or subcontractor duplicates in a subcontract with a lower-tier subcontractor. For example, let's say clause XYZ is in the prime contractor's government contract with US Department of Justice. If the prime contractor *flows down* clause XYZ by including it in a subcontract, clause XYZ is a *flow-down clause*. The prime contractor "flows down" clause XYZ from its own government contract to its subcontractor. Both the government contract (between Department of Justice and prime contractor) and the subcontract (between prime contractor and subcontractor) have some version of clause XYZ. Therefore, clause XYZ has *flowed down* to the subcontractor.

Why are flow-down clauses important for government contractors?

The inclusion or deletion of flow-down clauses will be a repeated subject of negotiations between your company and its prime contractors or subcontractors. Bad clauses can flow downstream! Be careful.

Prime contractors have an incentive — whether lazily or shrewdly — to include more flow-down clauses than necessary with their subcontractors. Likewise, higher tier subcontractors have an incentive to include more flow-down clauses than necessary with their lower tier subcontractors.

These risky, costly, or unnecessary flow-down clauses tend to flow downstream. Your company must negotiate and redline all of these unnecessary clauses for deletion. Otherwise, your company is accepting unnecessary risk as well as avoidable costs.

What guidance is there for when to use flow-down clauses?

Just like the prescription clause provides instructions, the *flow-down prescription clause* gives instructions to the prime contractor or subcontractor about when to include (to *flow down*) the same FAR clauses.

There is an important reason why flow-down prescription clauses must exist in the contract itself, and not merely in the FAR. The reason is that your company does not follow the FAR. Your company follows only what is in the government contract. For more information, read the chapter, "No, the FAR Does Not Apply to Government Contractors."

How does *privity of contract* relate to *flow-down clauses*?

The United States government has *privity of contract* (a direct contractual relationship) with the prime contractor only. The government has no privity or direct contractual relationship with any of the subcontractors. For more information on the concept of privity of contract, read the chapter, "Prime Contractors Versus Subcontractors."

The only way the government can ensure that FAR clauses included in the prime contract will be *flowed down* and inserted into the subcontracts is to force the prime contractor to do so. Of course, the best way to force the prime contractor to do anything is to include mandatory language in the prime contract. Your company follows this prime contract only, and not the FAR.

Naturally, this process is exactly what the government imposes on prime contractors. Many FAR clauses contain within themselves instructions to *flow down* the clause into any subcontracts. When your company signs the prime contract with the government, your company agrees to *flow down* the clause to all subcontractors.

How does the government ensure the prime contractor will flow down certain clauses within subcontracts?

If the government wants FAR clauses to flow down to subcontractors, the text of the FAR clause itself must include mandatory language to *flow down* the clause in subcontracts. It must be the FAR clause in the contract itself — not merely the instructions to contracting officers found in the FAR — because the FAR does not apply to government contractors. The FAR applies to federal employees conducting acquisitions, such as contracting officers. Review the chapter, "No, the FAR Does Not Apply to Government Contractors."

What is the relationship between flow-down clauses and prescription clauses?

Flow-down prescription clauses are found within the FAR clause itself and direct your company to include identical or similar FAR clauses in any related subcontracts.

The FAR prescription clause directs the contracting officer to include that clause in the prime contract. The text of the *flow-down prescription clause*, within the FAR clause found in the prime contract, directs the prime contractor to include that clause in subcontracts.

What dangerous clauses should you refuse and certainly never flow down to your subcontractors?

Do not flow down any version of this clause to your subcontractors:

> "The entire prime government contract is hereby incorporated into this subcontract. When the term "government" or "contracting officer" is used it shall mean [your company] or [your company's contract administrator], respectively. When the term "contractor" is used it shall mean subcontractor."

Never sign any contract or subcontract that includes wording like the above. You can see how this type of clause substitutes your company for the government and substitutes the subcontractor for your company.

In this way, your company becomes the government, and the entire prime contract with the government is somehow "incorporated into" the subcontract. This makes for an incoherent mess! Do not use this clause. Do not sign any contract or subcontract that includes such a clause. Instead, negotiate, edit, tailor, and *flow down* the clauses as they seem appropriate.

What is another example of a dangerous clause to never accept in your contract or subcontract?

Never flow down a clause like this:

> "The entire Federal Acquisition Regulation (FAR) and all of its clauses are hereby incorporated in full into this subcontract."

Again, this language creates a mess! The FAR contains conflicting instructions and clauses that cannot all apply to a single contract. Do not allow this clause. Do not sign any contract or subcontract that includes such a clause.

CHAPTER 5, THE MYTH OF SELF-DELETING CLAUSES

What is a self-deleting clause?

There is no such thing as a self-deleting clause. Be very careful with any "professionals" who talk about self-deleting clauses. The theory behind this hoax is that if any clause is inappropriate for the contract, it is somehow automatically "self-deleting." Therefore, you might not need to worry about the clause being written into the contract you have read and signed. This idea is absurd.

Do any clauses automatically disappear, like a magician's trick?

No, clauses do not automatically disappear. Are these clauses written with disappearing ink from a child's magic store? No. Does the page of the contract that contains the clause automatically self-destruct after 24 hours, like some James Bond movie? No. The clause remains in your contract for one and all to read.

Rather than magically disappearing, how can certain clauses be invalidated?

After litigation, some clauses might be found by a judge to be unenforceable, illegal, or otherwise rendered inoperative. (Read more about this concept in the chapter, "The Christian Doctrine and Missing Government Contract Clauses.") But to rely on the nonexistent legal principle of "self-deleting" clauses during negotiations is the unmistakable mark of an amateur.

What should I do if I see a clause that does not belong in my contract?

If you see a clause that does not belong in your contract, negotiate to delete that clause. Do not accept an explanation of how the clause self-deletes. If the clause is supposedly self-deleting anyway, why should your negotiation partner care if you delete it? Negotiate to delete these clauses.

What about the *Christian doctrine*?

The *Christian doctrine* is an important exception to the myth of self-deleting clauses. Although courts may magically *insert* into your contract certain, specific FAR clauses — even if the government forgets to include them before signature — a similar rule allows courts to magically *remove* from your contract certain, specific FAR clauses. So, the principle of the *Christian doctrine* has expanded from inserting missing FAR clauses on to removing or correcting incorrect FAR clauses. For more information, read the chapter, "The Christian Doctrine and Missing Government Contract Clauses."

Do not rely on the expanded *Christian doctrine* to validate the myth of self-deleting clauses. Whether the FAR clause is inserted, removed, or replaced, this action is a remedy imposed by a judge during litigation. The FAR clause is not "self-deleting." Rather, the same FAR clause is held to be inapplicable, inappropriate, or otherwise not valid by a judge in a court of law (or similar forum). This extraordinary remedy is rare and achieved only after painful and costly litigation. In contrast, the myth of the self-deleting clause misleads you into believing that the clause will painlessly fade into the background with no effort. Not true at all! You must in fact delete, manually, any and all clauses that do not belong in your contract.

CHAPTER 6, NO, THE FAR DOES NOT APPLY TO GOVERNMENT CONTRACTORS

Is the door closed? I'm going to share one of the biggest secrets in government contracting. Everyone in the government contracts world has heard of the Federal Acquisition Regulation or FAR. Some call it the "Bible" for government contracts. Are you sitting down? Take a deep breath, because I have some shocking news for you: *The FAR does not apply to government contractors!* I wrote a full-length article on this topic, and I'm happy to send it to you if you email Christoph@ChristophLLC.com. But here's the crisp summary for the busy executive.

Does the FAR apply to government contractors?

No, the FAR applies to the federal employees involved in acquisition, namely, the contracting officers. Think of the FAR as the book of instructions to contracting officers as to which FAR clauses to include in the contract. If you want proof, read FAR 1.104, which explains that the FAR applies to all acquisitions. "Acquisition," according to FAR 2.101, means "the acquiring by contract… by and for the use of the Federal Government." Case closed. The FAR applies to acquisitions conducted by the federal government. Therefore, the FAR applies only to federal employees, not to federal contractors.

Is the FAR important for federal contractors to understand?

Yes, the FAR is extremely important to federal contractors, but only insofar as their contracts include certain FAR clauses.

These FAR clauses are the connecting tissue between the government and the contractor. As such, individual FAR clauses must be included in the contract, or else they are not relevant (saving complicating factors like the *Christian* doctrine for another time). For more info, read the chapter, "The Christian Doctrine and Missing Government Contract Clauses."

Is the entire FAR incorporated into my government contract?

No, the entire FAR is not incorporated into your federal contract. That's not how things work. Instead, individual clauses are included on a case-by-case basis.

What should I do if someone sends me a FAR citation not found in my contract?

Do not fall for the bluff of a FAR citation that is not in your contract! Both the government contracting officer and your private sector negotiation partners will try to fool you, but do not fall for this common trick. You are reading my book. You know better! Follow your contract.

Why should I care if a FAR citation is found within my contract?

When you get a FAR citation, check immediately to see if that clause is in your contract. If that FAR clause is not found in your contract, why should you care about it? Is there a portion of your contract that incorporates that section of the FAR? If not, your opponent is blowing smoke.

Government contracting officers are infamous for attempting this trick. They hit you with a FAR citation and say "The FAR requires that you do this. Please comply." Now you know how to handle this ruse. Ask for the page number of your contract that requires you to comply. Be respectful and polite but stand your ground.

Should I follow my contract or the FAR?

You are bound by your individual contract terms, not by the FAR. If your contract references or incorporates sections or clauses of the FAR, then those specific sections or clauses of the FAR may apply to your company. When in doubt, read your contract carefully! If you need help, you can email me at Christoph@ChristophLLC.com.

CHAPTER 7, THE CHRISTIAN DOCTRINE AND MISSING GOVERNMENT CONTRACT CLAUSES

What is the *Christian* doctrine?

First, the *Christian* doctrine has nothing to do with Christianity or theology. The *Christian* doctrine is called a doctrine because a judge created it in a court of law. The name "Christian" comes from a famous court case involving a government contractor called G.L. Christian & Associates.

Is the *Christian* doctrine based on precedent?

Yes. The *Christian* doctrine is *precedent*, meaning a rule created by a judge that other judges follow in similar cases. This rule says that certain clauses from the Federal Acquisition Regulation (FAR) are so important that the court will pretend as though these clauses are in your government contract, even if the clauses are not actually in the contract you signed. If the *Christian* doctrine sounds unfair to you, you are paying attention.

When will the *Christian* doctrine apply?

The official test for the judge to use the *Christian* doctrine has two parts. The first part asks whether the FAR clause is mandatory. This question asks whether the *prescription clause* instructs the contracting officer to include the clause in the type of contract that your company signed with the government.

If the instructions ("prescription") for the clause provide wiggle room or discretion, or if your contract is not appropriate, then the first part of the _Christian_ doctrine fails. If the first or second part of the _Christian_ doctrine fails, the missing clause will not be magically inserted into your government contract.

The second part of the _Christian_ doctrine asks whether the FAR clause expresses a "significant" or "deeply ingrained strand" of government contracting policy. The interpretation of this second part is unpredictable and subjective. The judge gets to decide whether the FAR clause is so important that it cannot be left out of the government contract.

What is the summarized two-part test for applying the _Christian_ doctrine?

In summary, this test for applying the _Christian_ doctrine has two parts. If either part fails, then the judge cannot magically include the missing FAR clause into your government contract.

Part 1. The FAR clause has mandatory instructions to the contracting officer that require its inclusion in the type of government contract you signed.

Part 2. The FAR clause is considered to express a "significant" or "deeply ingrained strand" of government contracting policy. This decision is extremely subjective.

Does the _Christian_ doctrine apply to subcontracts?

No, the _Christian_ doctrine does not apply to subcontracts or any contracts between two businesses. It applies only to prime contracts of your company with the government.

What if the government contracting officer brings up the _Christian_ doctrine?

Congratulations, your company has already won the argument if the contracting officer starts talking about the _Christian_ doctrine.

Why do you say my company already wins the argument if the contracting officer brings up the _Christian_ doctrine?

The contracting officer forgot to include the FAR clause in your government contract. Months or years later, the contracting officer wants to use this FAR clause against your company, but the FAR clause is not in the contract. Your company points out that this FAR clause is not in the government contract. The contracting officer responds by saying, "Due to the _Christian_ doctrine, this FAR clause is included in the contract by operation of law. You must comply with this FAR clause."

So, the contracting officer thinks you will give up because the gambit of the _Christian_ doctrine sounds legitimate. Do not fall for this bluff! The contracting officer is not a judge.

Who enforces the _Christian_ doctrine?

Remember that the _Christian_ doctrine is created and enforced by judges in courts of law. This means the bluffing contracting officer imagines that two things will happen. First, your company and the government will sue each other and end up in court. Second, the court will apply the _Christian_ doctrine and magically insert the missing FAR clause into your contract. There is a strong chance, however, that one or both things will not happen.

What should I say to the contracting officer during a _Christian_ doctrine situation?

Remind the contracting officer that it will require expensive and time-consuming litigation to get a judge to use the _Christian_ doctrine against your company. The smarter solution is to negotiate in good faith to include the missing clause in your government contract. The government also owes your company extra money to comply with the new FAR clause. Make sure you negotiate a modification that inserts the new FAR clause into the old contract and gives your company more money, if appropriate. For advice with this process, read the chapter, "How to Ask for More Money: REAs versus Claims."

Is there a list of _Christian_ doctrine clauses?

No, there is no list. There cannot be an exhaustive, official, and complete list because the _Christian_ doctrine is created and enforced by judges in courts of law. Therefore, the list can always expand when the next judge applies the _Christian_ doctrine to a new FAR clause.

However, there are FAR clauses that judges have ruled are covered under the _Christian_ doctrine. These FAR clauses include Disputes, Changes, Termination, and others. Just remember that no list will be complete because a new FAR clause can always enter the mix after a new court case.

CHAPTER 8, HOW TO RESEARCH ANY FAR CLAUSE

How is the FAR organized?

The Federal Acquisition Regulation (FAR) is organized into 53 "parts." For example, FAR Part 19 covers Small Business Programs. FAR Part 6 covers Competition Requirements. FAR Part 52 contains all the standard contract clauses and solicitation provisions.

How should I research FAR clauses?

First, read this entire chapter to learn the "secret code" of interpreting every single FAR clause. By interpreting the numbers in your FAR clauses, you can tell exactly which part of the FAR explains the policy behind that clause, giving you important context and background.

If you are not comfortable performing an analysis of *every* FAR clause, term, condition, word, phrase, and requirement in *each* of your government contracts, send me an email at Christoph@ChristophLLC.com. I perform such executive summaries for my clients. Maybe I will do it for you!

When researching FAR clauses, why should you always read the scope, applicability, and definitions sections?

You need to understand each FAR section within its broader context or else you will make serious mistakes. You can discover the context by first researching the scope, applicability, and definitions sections that correspond to the FAR citation. You can remember this research method because scope, applicability, and definitions form the acronym "SAD." You can call this the *SAD method*.

Should you read individual sections of the FAR — or sections of your contract — in complete isolation?

No! The FAR is complicated because you cannot read a section of the FAR in isolation by itself. Regulations like the FAR must be read "as a whole," with each section harmonized with other sections. (The same principle applies to contract interpretation; contracts must be read "as a whole" and harmonized.) The easiest way to properly understand a FAR citation is to read the scope, applicability, and definitions section before you read the specific FAR language in question.

What context is provided by the FAR sections of scope, applicability, and definitions (SAD)?

Within the FAR, many different sections are dedicated to scope, applicability, and definitions. These special sections apply to some specific FAR sections, but not to the entire FAR. These special sections provide guidance about how to read and understand those specific sections of the FAR, but that guidance does not apply to the entire FAR. These special sections apply only in limited areas of the FAR.

For example, the scope section in FAR Part 19 applies to FAR Part 19, Small Business Programs only. There is an applicability section that applies to FAR Part 6, Competition Requirements only. Similarly, there is a definitions section that applies to FAR Subpart 33.1, Protests only. In each of these examples, the scope, applicability, and definitions section apply to no other sections of the FAR.

How will first reading the scope, applicability, and definitions sections inform your understanding of a FAR citation?

You should read the scope, applicability, and definitions sections (all three) before you try to analyze a specific section or citation of the FAR. Follow the *SAD method*.

By first reading the scope section, you gain a general understanding of the topic. By first reading the applicability section, you will know if you have an inaccurate citation that might not apply to your circumstances. By reading the definitions section first, you will find out whether certain words have special meanings within the larger FAR citation. The *SAD method* — first checking the scope, applicability, and definitions sections — is critical to researching and understanding the FAR properly.

What can you learn from the scope section?

The scope section provides a bird's-eye view of the FAR citation. Each FAR part starts with a scope section. Some of the FAR subparts have their own scope sections as well. Just remember that each scope section applies only to the FAR part, subpart, or section that it specifies. For example, you cannot apply a scope section from FAR Part 25 to FAR citations from FAR Part 26.

The scope section has background information or context for the FAR citation and larger FAR section. For example, the scope section for FAR Part 19, Small Business Programs, informs us that this part involves aspects of the Small Business Act, such as small business set-asides.

What can you learn from the applicability section?

The applicability section has vital information about the relevance of the larger FAR part, subpart, or section. The applicability section answers the question, "Does this FAR citation apply to my current situation?"

Some applicability sections give you clear exemptions or exceptions. For example, the applicability section for FAR Part 6, Competition Requirements tells you that the competition requirements do not apply to simplified acquisition procedures. This is need-to-know information. Ignorance of the applicability sections causes many mistakes. Reading the applicability sections can help you avoid unnecessary trouble.

When you question whether you need to consider the substance of a FAR citation, the first place to look is the applicability section. It just might be your get-out-of-jail-free card.

What can you learn from the definitions section?

The definitions section of each FAR part, subpart, or section provides special definitions that only apply in that FAR part, subpart, or section. The most popular definitions section is in FAR Part 2, Definitions of Words of Terms. However—and this is a very important however—there are many other definitions sections throughout the FAR. The number of distinct definitions sections in the FAR is in the double digits. Think that over, and never forget it.

The definitions section in FAR Part 2 defines words and terms that are used frequently in the FAR. You can consider the definitions in FAR Part 2 to be "universal" or "general" definitions. Just do not forget all the other definition sections.

In summary, when researching any FAR clause or citation, first refer to the relevant scope, applicability, and definitions sections to gain a wider perspective of the context.

Where are all FAR contract clauses located?

FAR Part 52 contains all the standard FAR clauses.

Where are all FAR solicitation provisions located?

FAR Part 52 contains all the standard FAR provisions.

What is the difference between a clause and provision?

Clauses go in the *contract*. Provisions go in the *solicitation*. Therefore, we call them *contract clauses* and *solicitation provisions*.

There may be some overlap, such as when a contract clause is found in both the solicitation and resulting contract, but that overlap is to give every potential contractor notice that the clause will apply. If you see the contract clause in the solicitation, that inclusion indicates any resulting contract will also include that clause.

Is there a pattern or "secret code" to the numbering of all FAR clauses?

Yes, a simple pattern or "secret code" applies to all FAR clauses, telling you the origin and purpose of each FAR clause. Continue reading to learn the secret code!

Why does every FAR clause start with the number 52?

Every FAR clause starts with 52 because all FAR clauses are found in FAR Part 52.

What do the numbers after 52 signify?

After the number 52, every FAR clause has a period or dot, then three numbers, then a dash, then more numbers. Pay attention to the first three numbers after the period.

Of those three numbers, the first will be the number two. That first detail is not important. But the second and third numbers tell you something important about the FAR clause.

What is the secret code of all FAR clause numbers?

If the FAR clause starts with 52.219, that clause derives from FAR Part 19, Small Business Programs. Ignore the 52 and ignore the number two after the period. You are left with 19, which tells you that FAR clause comes from FAR Part 19. Another example is a FAR clause that starts with 52.249. Any FAR clause that starts with 52.249 derives from FAR Part 49, Terminations. You just learned the secret code to research any FAR clause!

Why should I care about the FAR Part that corresponds to the FAR clause?

Each FAR clause has specific directions to the contracting officer about when to insert the clause. This detail helps you understand the purpose of the FAR clause and gives you negotiating leverage if you want to remove it before signing the contract.

How can I follow changes or updates to the FAR?

All federal regulations, including the FAR, must follow the "public notice and comment" process. This process gives the public advanced, written notice of new and changing regulations and it allows the public to write comments or opinions or objections to send to the regulators.

You can follow changes to federal regulations at the *Federal Register* website. The *Federal Register* posts upcoming proposed and final changes to regulations like the FAR. For most changes to the FAR, you can rely on the secondary reporting and analysis of professionals like Christoph LLC. Email Christoph@ChristophLLC.com to sign up for my monthly free newsletter of important updates in government contracting.

Many law firms and consulting companies publish online articles and updates about major changes to the FAR. You can usually read these for free on the Internet. If you attend government contracting conferences, you can learn the latest and greatest from experts and insiders while you expand your network of potential teaming partners.

Why does the FAR exist?

Before the FAR, several different sets of government contracting regulations existed. One applied to defense contracts. Another applied to contracts with the National Aeronautics and Space Administration. A third set of regulations applied to contracts with all other federal agencies. This arrangement was confusing. In 1984, the FAR was created to create a single set of federal regulations for all government contracts. The FAR replaced the three previous sets of regulations.

What about agency supplements like the DFARS?

Of course, the simplicity of having one set of government contracting regulations did not last. "Nothing gold can stay." Various federal agencies started creating their own, additional, distinct regulations. These regulations supplement (but do not replace) the FAR, so they are called *agency supplements*.

The Department of Defense issues the *Defense FAR Supplement* or *DFARS*. The US Air Force issues the *Air Force FAR Supplement* or *AFFARS*. Scores of other federal agencies issue agency supplements.

Will my government contract contain both FAR clauses and agency supplement clauses?

Yes, possibly. Your government contracts may contain clauses from the FAR and also from agency supplements. If you work with defense agencies, you might have to deal with three sets of regulations. For example, a government contract with the Air Force may contain clauses from the FAR, the DFARS, and the AFFARS.

What does "incorporate by reference" mean?

Incorporate by reference means your contract lists the number and title of the FAR clause, but not the full text of the clause. Your contract may include more than one hundred FAR clauses. The full text of so many FAR clauses will take up valuable space in the contract. Instead of including the full text, the contracting officer can "incorporate by reference" some of the FAR clauses.

For example, you may see a single line in your contract that states:

"FAR 52.243-1   Changes, Fixed-Price (Aug 1987)"

Even though the contracting officer did not include the full text of FAR 52.243-1, you are responsible for following the full text of FAR 52.243-1. Incorporating a clause by reference saves space and makes the contract easier to read. However, you must be careful because you remain responsible for the entirety of whatever FAR clause is incorporated by reference.

What does "incorporate by full text" mean?

Incorporate by full text means the contracting officer includes the complete text of the FAR clause in your contract. You will see the number and title of the FAR clause as well as a paragraph or more underneath, consisting of the full text of the clause.

CHAPTER 9, ALTERNATE VERSIONS OF FAR CLAUSES

What does "ALT" or "alternate" signify in the title of a FAR clause?

Some FAR clauses have alternate versions to use for different circumstances, although the substance or topic of each clause remains the same. For example, there are several alternate versions for the Changes clause for cost-reimbursement contracts. The alternate versions apply depending on whether the contract is for services, supplies, or construction. Yet all versions are Changes clauses that apply to the cost-reimbursement contracts.

What does the date after the FAR clause mean?

You may notice the FAR clauses in your contract have a date, shown usually within parentheses, after the number and title. Just as the rest of the FAR is updated constantly, FAR clauses are also frequently updated. Therefore, the date after the FAR clause refers to the last update to that FAR clause. The date is referred to as the *version* of the FAR clause to distinguish it from earlier or later revisions of the same FAR clause.

What if my FAR clause does not include a date after the number and title?

The contracting officer should always include a date after the number and title, so this omission indicates a mistake or oversight. In this case, you should be responsible to perform the latest version of that FAR clause that exists on the date you signed the contract. Finding out which version applies may require intense research into previous or archived FAR editions.

When a FAR clause referenced in my contract is updated and replaced by a newer version, but my contract did not change, do my responsibilities under the contract change?

No, not if your contract has not changed, and this point is important for you to remember. You negotiated a deal when you signed the government contract. The bargain included the FAR clauses in the contract as of the date you signed the contract. You cannot be responsible for constantly changing clauses. Your company is responsible for the versions of the FAR clauses in the contract as indicated by their dates. In the absence of specified dates, however, you may be responsible for the latest versions of the FAR clauses in effect at the time you signed the contract.

What if the contracting officer wants to update one or more FAR clauses in my contract to newer versions?

Changing a FAR clause changes your responsibilities under the contract. Changing your responsibilities under the contract may cause your company to spend more time and money. Therefore, changing any FAR clause may entitle your company to an *equitable adjustment*. In plain English, an *equitable adjustment* means your company gets more money, a schedule extension, or some other type of contractual relief.

Can the contracting officer update my FAR clauses when exercising the option?

Yes, but by changing the FAR clauses, the government loses its right to exercise the option unilaterally (without your permission). Your company agreed to perform the option period when it signed the contract, but your company did not agree to the updates to the FAR clause. The contracting officer must separate these modifications to retain the right to exercise your option unilaterally.

Although the contracting officer can combine the option exercise with other changes, this combination means your company may be entitled to an *equitable adjustment*, meaning money, schedule extensions, or some other contractual relief. Also, because the modification authority is no longer unilateral, your company can choose to "walk away" and decline performance of the option.

CHAPTER 10, NOTEWORTHY FAR CLAUSES

What are the most impactful or noteworthy FAR clauses?

You should pay special attention to Federal Acquisition Regulation (FAR) clauses that deal with these topics: changes, terminations, delivery, inspection, acceptance, limitations on subcontracting, and certified cost or pricing data. These critical clauses should come first when you review your government contract. If one of the following clauses is in your government contract, take the time to read the complete clause or hire a professional to walk you through it.

What is the Changes clause?

Several versions of the *Changes clause* allow the government to change contracts unilaterally, but within certain limits. These limits depend on which version of the Changes clause exists in your contract. Contracting officers use different versions of the Changes clause based upon factors such as (1) whether your contract is fixed price or cost reimbursement and (2) whether your company provides supplies or services.

The biggest wildcard for any government contract is the Changes clause. Most contracts establish the rights and responsibilities of the parties while providing a specific task to perform or product to deliver. Sometimes the contract includes a Statement of Work (SOW) or specifications to follow. Most contracts allow your company to foresee exactly what it must do to fulfill the contract. The Changes clause turns that concept on its head.

Can you decline performance of a modification under the Changes clause?

No. At any time, the government contracting officer can send you a modification to the contract pursuant to the Changes clause. This message will not be a negotiation. Your company cannot decline the modification. Instead, by signing the original contract including the Changes clause, your company has already agreed to such unilateral changes! If the Changes clause sounds unfair to you as the contractor, you have paid attention to my advice.

Does the Changes clause allow for any type of changes to the contract?

No. Never forget that the Changes clause does not give authority to the government to make unlimited changes. These changes must exactly match the same changes listed in your version of the Changes clause. Most versions of the Changes clause allow unilateral changes to such matters as product specifications, services for delivery, and place of performance or delivery.

Will you get paid for extra costs to adapt to modifications under the Changes clause?

Yes, you are entitled to payment. The Changes clause does not require your company to work for free. Changes cost money and the government is required to compensate your company. When the contracting officer sends your company a unilateral modification pursuant to the Changes clause, your first thought should be to calculate the cost of compliance. Then you need to get paid by submitting a request for equitable adjustment (REA) or claim under the Contract Disputes Act. For more information, read the chapter, "How to Ask for More Money: REAs versus Claims."

What is a termination clause?

The phrase *termination clause* doesn't sound very appealing, does it? Death, destruction, ending, finality, time-traveling cybernetic organisms with Austrian accents!

You may be familiar with termination clauses in your apartment lease or cell phone contract. When you want to move early or switch cell phone providers, you will read your termination clauses to determine your rights and how to proceed.

How does a termination clause work in government contracting?

In government contracting, the *termination clauses* allow the government to fire or terminate your company abruptly. You need to understand the three types of termination clauses: *convenience*, *default*, and *cause*.

What is the scariest clause in all of government contracting?

The scariest clause in all of government contracting is *Termination for Convenience of the Government*. This clause allows the government to fire or terminate your company abruptly without paying the rest of the money from the remaining contract. To put this in perspective, let's contrast it with private sector contracts.

You sign a contract with Donald Trump for $500 million worth of supplies across 5 years, $100 million per year. Your company provides the supplies, Donald Trump provides the $500 million. At the end of the first year, Donald Trump delivers his famous line, "You're fired!" There is no reason for the termination. It occurs simply for the convenience of The Donald.

Under private sector contract law, can you sue for your missing profits?

Yes. In private sector contract law, you are entitled now to sue Donald Trump for at least some of the remaining money on the contract. You spent millions of dollars preparing for this 5-year contract. You hired hundreds of professionals.

By breaking the deal and violating the contract, The Donald harmed your company or deprived it of future revenue. You can sue The Donald for this future revenue – it's called *expectation damages*. Expectation damages can be thought of as the dollars you expected to receive if The Donald had carried the terms of the contract rightfully to their conclusion.

Under government contract law and the Termination clause, can you sue for your missing profits?

No. Contrast this private sector example involving The Donald with the frightening realm of government contracting. Instead of The Donald, you sign a government contract with the Department of Justice for $500 million worth of services over 5 years, $100 million per year. At the end of the first year, the Department of Justice contracting officer writes you an email that states: "You are hereby terminated for the convenience of the government." Guess what? You cannot sue the government or Department of Justice for any loss of future revenue. You can try, but you will lose. You are not entitled to the *expectation damages* of the broken deal.

Now you see the reasoning behind why the *Termination for Convenience of the Government* is the scariest clause in government contracting. Although you can get paid for a few things after your company is terminated for convenience, you are not entitled to *expectation damages*. Aside from some minor costs your company incurred to wind down the contract, the government walks away from your disaster with zero liability. This extraordinary power of the government can bankrupt your company.

Is the Termination clause part of the "cost of doing business" with the federal government?

Terminations for convenience are a risk that almost every government contractor incurs, whether knowingly or in ignorance. You must price in the risk of these terminations for your long-term business plans. Every day the sun comes up is another day for the government to terminate your entire contract and pay your company nothing for breaking the deal. Technically, the "deal" or contract says the government can do this and your company agrees!

If my prime contract contains the Termination for Convenience clause, should I include something similar in any subcontracts?

Yes, you should! If your prime contract with the government has the *Termination for Convenience of the Government clause*, you need to *flow down* a version of this clause to your subcontractors. If you do not do so, then the government can terminate your prime contract while you are still on the hook to pay all your subcontractors. Remember, your subcontractors can sue you for *expectation damages*. You will be left holding the bag when the government terminates your company for convenience.

To avoid this disaster, include a Termination for Convenience clause flow-down in your subcontracts. Stipulate that your company can use the Termination for Convenience clause against the subcontractor if the government uses the Termination for Convenience clause against your company.

What if my company is the subcontractor performing work for a prime contractor?

If your company is the subcontractor, you should check your subcontract to see if the prime contractor has the right to terminate your company for convenience. If so, you should negotiate to change the subcontract terms to allow the prime contractor to terminate your company *only if* the government terminates the prime contractor.

In other words, do not give any prime contractor the discretion to terminate your subcontract for convenience. Allow the prime contractor to terminate your company only to comply with a termination by the government. Include a requirement for the prime contractor to show proof of this termination.

What is the Termination for Cause clause?

When the government procures commercial items (which can be products or services), the government is supposed to use a different clause that does not allow terminations for *default*. Commercial government contracts should include a clause that allows for terminations *for cause*.

Terminations for cause in commercial government contracts must be based on some failure of your company. This process differs completely from the scary *Termination for Convenience of the Government clause*. Contract language about termination for cause is nothing to lose sleep over, but being terminated for cause is a nightmare! You can read more about terminations for default to understand why you must avoid terminations for cause or for default.

What is the Termination for Default clause?

In noncommercial government contracts, the contracting officer is supposed to use a version of the Termination clause that allows for termination *for default*. Just like the commercial version (termination *for cause*), any termination *for default* requires some failure of your company — hence the word *default*. Your company has *defaulted* on its responsibility to fulfill the contract.

If your company is *terminated for default*, this termination may be a death sentence. The termination for default will appear on your company record for years. Other potential government clients will review this information before they decide to award you a contract. At all costs your company must avoid being terminated by default.

If my company is terminated for default, can I fight back in any way?

One way to dodge a termination for default is to convert the bitter pill into a termination for convenience.

When government contractors litigate or challenge terminations for default, they're sometimes settled, transformed, or ruled by a judge to be a termination for convenience. This change saves the company's reputation within government contracting. That outcome is what your company wants, so try to negotiate a termination for convenience rather than a termination for default.

What are the warning signs that the government plans to terminate my contract?

The government may send you two warning signs before terminating your company. If you see any correspondence with the words *Cure Notice* or *Show Cause*, you need to go on red alert. Assemble your company's chain of command and get in touch with your expert for government contracting.

What is a *Cure Notice*?

The *Cure Notice* provides your company a written warning that something is wrong. Your company is doing something or failing to do something that may breach the contract and result in a termination for default.

What will the language look like in an official *Cure Notice* from the government?

Cure Notice language will read something like this:

"You are notified that the Government considers your ____ [specify the contractor's failure or failures] a condition that is endangering performance of the contract. Therefore, unless this condition is cured within 10 days after receipt of this notice [or insert any longer time that the Contracting Officer may consider reasonably necessary], the Government may terminate for default under the terms and conditions of the _____ [insert clause title] clause of this contract."

What is a *Show Cause Notice*?

Show Cause is a more urgent notice that your company may soon be terminated for default. It warns your company to spell out any reasons why the government should not terminate you for default. Usually the *Cure Notice* comes before the *Show Cause Notice*, which comes just before your oncoming termination for default. Receiving a *Show Cause Notice* is like hearing the ominous question, "Any last words?" or "What do you want on your tombstone?" It is your last opportunity for rescue before termination.

What is so important about delivery, inspection, and acceptance clauses?

Strictly adhering to clauses related to delivery, inspection, and acceptance will determine whether your company succeeds or spirals into a costly failure. Scan your contract for anything related to delivery, inspection, and acceptance (or refusal). You need to know when, where, and how to deliver the supplies or services your contract requires. Before you sign the contract, make sure you understand precisely how you must deliver. This analysis is not limited to supplies.

What should you consider for services contracts?

If your government contract is for services, you also need to know where and when to perform the services. Do you need access to a military base or government-owned building? Do your employees need security clearances? Will your employees need to follow a schedule set by the government rather than your own company management? Will your company be paid for time during federal holidays, when the government is closed and when workers are not occupied?

Can inspection and acceptance delay your payment?

Yes. For you to be paid, first your company must deliver. Then the government inspects and accepts. Keep in mind that inspection and acceptance is not always performed by the same person or even the same office. You need to have some idea of how the government will inspect and accept whatever your company provides under the contract. What factors lead to a success or failure during inspection? Will everything be inspected or just a test sample only? How much time can the government take during inspection? How long can the government wait before pronouncing acceptance or rejection of the delivery?

Such questions can make or break a government contract. Details of delivery, inspection, and acceptance are vital. Do not be afraid to ask questions about these topics. Carefully read and analyze all sections of the contract that deal with delivery, inspection, or acceptance.

What are the Limitations on Subcontracting clauses?

The *Limitations on Subcontracting clauses* strictly control how much and to whom you can subcontract work under your prime contract with the government.

When the government awards your company a contract, it wants your specific company to perform most of the contract. Your company cannot subcontract away too much of the work, depending on the situation. This simple principle is enforced by the *Limitations on Subcontracting clauses*. There are several versions of this clause, and the clause operates differently depending on the specific type of contract, but this chapter provides the basics.

What is the policy goal behind the Limitations on Subcontracting clauses?

Small business set-asides are supposed to benefit small businesses. Women-owned small business set-asides are supposed to benefit women-owned small businesses. This policy is easy to understand.

If the government awards a small business set-aside to a small business that subcontracts 90 percent of the work to a large company like Boeing, something is probably wrong. Boeing gets the benefit of the set-aside instead of the small business. For this reason, specific limitations exist on how much your company can subcontract after it receives a set-aside.

Is there more than one version of the Limitations on Subcontracting clause?

Yes, there are several versions of the Limitations on Subcontracting clause. You must know which version of the clause is in your contract. Pay attention to the date at the end of the title of the clause. Over time, these clauses do change. Although the title may be the same, the substance of a clause can change.

How much of the prime contract must my company perform when subject to one of the Limitations on Subcontracting clauses?

Again, each version of the Limitations on Subcontracting clause differs slightly. There are differing percentage limitations and differing ways to calculate the percentage. Some calculate based on money paid to employees, some allow contractors to subtract the cost of materials, and some examine total contract values rather than company expenses. Generally, these Limitations on Subcontracting clauses prohibit your company from subcontracting away more than 50 percent or one-half of the contract.

Sometimes the percentage limitation is greater than 50 percent. In those cases, your company can subcontract away more work. For example, construction contracts have more flexibility because it's common for complex construction projects to have many different subcontractors.

Should my company consider the Limitations on Subcontracting clauses in its teaming agreements?

Yes, when your company negotiates and signs teaming agreements to work together with other government contractors, beware the Limitations on Subcontracting clauses. Beware companies that offer subcontractors to perform more than 50 percent of the work for set-aside prime contracts. Such companies may promise more than they can deliver.

Your teaming agreement exists between your company and the other contractor, but the government may cause problems. If the government enforces the Limitations on Subcontracting against the prime contractor, the prime contractor may choose to violate the teaming agreement to satisfy the government. Avoid messy situations by anticipating which version of the Limitations on Subcontracting clause will apply to the prime contractor.

Does the Limitations on Subcontracting clause apply to all government contracts?

No, the Limitations on Subcontracting clause does not apply to government contracts that are not set aside for small businesses. However, some similar limitations often apply to any other government contract.

What is the Limitations on Pass-Through Charges clause?

The *Limitations on Pass-Through Charges clause* is similar to the Limitations on Subcontracting clause. The difference is that the Limitations on Pass-Through Charges clause can be inserted into government contracts that are not set asides for small businesses.

How is the Limitations on Pass-Through Charges clause similar to the Limitations on Subcontract clause?

The similarity between the two clauses is that they both create strict limitations on how much work the prime contractor can subcontract. A second similarity is that both clauses enforce the government expectation that any company that receives a contract will perform a significant amount of the work.

What is the policy goal for the Limitations on Pass-Through Charges clause?

The Limitations on Pass-Through Charges clause prevents a prime contractor from getting the government to pay for the middleman. In this discussion, the "middleman" does not provide value and collects fees only by connecting the government to a lower tier subcontractor.

The government expects some subcontracting, but it does not want to pay excessive fees to middleman government contractors. This is the purpose of the Limitations on Pass-Through Charges clause.

Always read the specific language of this clause, which generally requires the prime contractor to report to the contracting officer if any subcontractor will perform more than 70 percent of the work. It also requires a report if any lower tier subcontractor will perform more than 70 percent of the work of the higher tier subcontractor.

The Limitations on Pass-Through Charges clause prohibits the government from paying "excessive" pass-through charges. The trigger for investigating whether pass-through charges are "excessive" is any subcontract for more than 70 percent of the work.

Is 70 percent automatically considered "excessive" pass-through charges?

No, not necessarily. You must distinguish between the threshold for notification (70 percent) and the prohibition on paying "excessive" pass-through charges.

"Excessive" is a relative and subjective term. The government contracting officer will determine whether the pass-through charges are excessive. Sometimes the government will pay pass-through charges if the contracting officer determines they are not excessive.

What is so important about clauses about submission of certified cost or pricing data?

Clauses related to your requirement to submit *certified cost or pricing data* create extra work to perform and also expose your company to significant risks.

What is TINA?

TINA is the *Truth in Negotiations Act*. Congress passed a law that became known as the Truth in Negotiations Act to give the government a huge advantage in sole-source negotiations. Since there is no competition, the government requires the contractor to disclose the "cost or pricing data" associated with the final cost or price. This disclosure is like playing poker with your cards facing up on the table. This disclosure of cost or pricing data allows the government to look at your proprietary financial information to pressure you into a lower cost or price. If the cost or pricing data is certified, you expose your company to a significant amount of risk, so these situations should be avoided whenever possible.

Why did Congress pass TINA to level the playing field when negotiating with large defense contractors?

Large defense contractors have billions of dollars and hundreds or thousands of highly paid employees. These defense contractors can run rings around the government contracting officers and program managers. There is no comparison if one side has 30 players while the other side has 3.

How did the government level the playing field against large defense contractors?

To level the playing field, Congress passed a law that became known as the Truth in Negotiations Act or TINA. If there is competition, meaning two or more contractors, the government can assume the invisible hand of the free market pushes prices down to a competitive level. However, in a sole-source negotiation, a contractor has significantly more power to determine pricing. TINA diminishes that power.

Is there another name for TINA?

Yes, the Truth in Negotiations Act (TINA) was later renamed the Truthful Cost or Pricing Data Act. Most people refer to it with the original name, "TINA."

What does TINA require my company to disclose?

TINA requires the contractor to disclose "cost or pricing data" and to certify the data in certain circumstances. The government uses this information to negotiate with the contractor. Let's be clear in this matter. No company would disclose this proprietary financial information (cost or pricing data) voluntarily. This deal is bad for the contractor, but it is a significant advantage to the government.

What is cost or pricing data?

In plain English, *cost or pricing data* means all facts that a reasonable businessman would expect to affect the cost or price negotiations. Remember that key word, "facts." These facts are different from the actual price or cost.

How does the Federal Acquisition Regulation define cost or pricing data?

Let's read the Federal Acquisition Regulation (FAR) definition:

> "Cost or pricing data" (10 U.S.C. 2306a(h)(1) and 41 U.S.C. chapter 35) means all facts that, as of the date of price agreement, or, if applicable, an earlier date agreed upon between the parties that is as close as practicable to the date of agreement on price, prudent buyers and sellers would reasonably expect to affect price negotiations significantly. Cost or pricing data are factual, not judgmental; and are verifiable. While they do not indicate the accuracy of the prospective contractor's judgment about estimated future costs or projections, they do include the data forming the basis for that judgment. Cost or pricing data are more than historical accounting data; they are all the facts that can be reasonably expected to contribute to the soundness of estimates of future costs and to the validity of determinations of costs already incurred."

There's a lot to unpack in that definition. Many lawsuits or claims have explored what is or is not cost or pricing data.

What are some practical examples of cost or pricing data?

Here are some practical examples of cost or pricing data:

Vendor quotations.

Nonrecurring costs.

Info on changes in production methods or purchasing volume.

Data supporting projections of business prospects or objectives.

Unit-cost trends such as those associated with labor efficiency.

Make-or-buy decisions.

Estimated resources to attain business goals.

Info on management decisions that significantly affect costs.

Does my cost or pricing data determine my actual price?

No! This misconception is all too common. The cost or pricing data consists of facts that a reasonable businessman would want to know because they would affect the negotiations. You are required to disclose these facts to the government.

You are not required to base your price on these facts (or on the cost or pricing data)! In other words, your complete cost or pricing data could lead a reasonable businessman to think that the price should be $1 million, including a tolerable profit of 20 percent. That does not mean your price must be $1 million. You can include a much higher profit and price and ask for $2 million or $20 million!

Are you saying I can price my proposal however I want, regardless of what my company submits as certified cost or pricing data?

Yes, you can price your proposal however you want. If you want to price your proposal using some other method, including methods not found in or associated with the cost or pricing data, you can do so!

You can even price your proposal using strange or arbitrary methods. The government might find that strange, but you can do it! Of course, if your method or pricing is unreasonable, there is no guarantee that the government will accept it.

What does "other than certified cost or pricing data" mean?

Sometimes the contractor has an exemption such that it does not have to provide certified cost or pricing data. In these cases, the contracting officer may still request *other than certified cost or pricing data*. This is precisely the same information, except that your company is not required to certify the information. If this sounds like a strangely convenient benefit the government created for itself, you're on the right track.

Does my company have to submit cost or pricing data?

No, you can always refuse to submit. However, in such a case the government is likely to decline awarding you the contract.

When you are in a sole-source negotiation for a government contract, you have a lot of leverage. You are the only potential contractor. Therefore, you might be able to get away with refusing to disclose any cost or pricing data, despite what the laws and regulations require of the contracting officer.

There are also waiver procedures for the contracting officer to give your company a pass or exception to providing cost or pricing data. You are not guaranteed to get a waiver or pass. Nor are you guaranteed to get the government contract. You must analyze your competitive negotiation position and decide whether to play nice. If you push things too far, you might lose the government contract.

What is so dangerous about certified cost or pricing data?

When an employee of your company *certifies* the cost or pricing data, it creates significant risk. If the cost or pricing data is wrong or *defective*, the government can "claw back" or demand money back from your company. Your company also risks being accused of submitting a *false claim*, which is a serious charge.

For these reasons, you should always consult a competent government contracting expert when you are making decisions about certified cost or pricing data. It is also important to know the rules of whether you need to submit cost or pricing data. If you are not a rules expert, you need to hire one.

What are the exceptions for submitting certified cost or pricing data?

Laws and regulations establish several exceptions to the requirement of submitting certified cost or pricing data. If you can prove one of these exceptions, your company is legitimately excused for not providing the data.

What is the exception for adequate price competition?

If there were a competition, or the expectation of competition, then this competition is not "sole source," and your company does not need to submit certified cost or pricing data. The actual definition of "adequate price competition" is multifaceted and complex. Check each possibility of adequate price competition to see if your company can use it.

What is the exception for commercial items?

Just like with adequate price competition, the definitions (plural!) of commercial items are complex. Both products and services may qualify as commercial items.

If you are delivering a commercial product or service to the government, you do not need to disclose certified cost or pricing data. It is very common for the government and contractor to disagree about whether a product or service is properly classified as commercial. Unfortunately, the person who makes the official determination of commerciality is the government contracting officer.

What is the exception for prices set by law or regulation?

If Congress or federal agencies have defined the prices, your company does not need to provide certified cost or pricing data. For example, sometimes the prices of utilities like electricity or water are defined by law or regulation.

What is the process of obtaining a waiver?

Your company's last shot is to obtain a waiver, in writing, from the government. This requires the signature of a high-level government official. That means you may have to go "over the head" of the contracting officer. Be careful about asking for this exception to submitting certified cost or pricing data. You do not want to antagonize the contracting officer!

Can you provide a strategic analysis and executive summary of the important clauses, terms, and conditions in all my government contracts?

Maybe. Ask for my help by sending an email to Christoph@ChristophLLC.com.

CHAPTER 11, CAST OF CHARACTERS

To become an effective negotiator, you must understand the cast of characters in government contracting. Definitely distinguish the positions and titles in the federal government versus those in industry. We can start with the federal government. If anything in this chapter is news to you, get the help you need by emailing me at Christoph@ChristophLLC.com.

Who is in the cast of characters representing my government client?

Most government contracts will involve a contracting officer, a contracting officer's representative (COR), and a program manager. To be an effective negotiator, you need to understand the titles and responsibilities of your government clients.

Who is the contracting officer?

Contracting officers have the authority to sign, administer, and terminate contracts on behalf of the federal government. They also have the authority to make such determinations as whether a product is specifically considered "commercial" or whether to exercise the next option year period of the contract. For prime contracts with the government, you will negotiate with a contracting officer.

What is a contracting officer's warrant?

The contracting officer's authority is specified by a *warrant*, which is a document defining the dollar value and types of government contracts the contracting officer has the authority to sign.

For example, one contracting officer may have a warrant to sign contracts up to $10 million. Another may have a $500 million warrant. An unlimited warrant generally bears no dollar limit. Some warrants are limited to government contracts rather than grants, and others allow for the signature of any type of government acquisition or assistance agreement, including procurement contracts, grants, cooperative agreements, and "Other Transactions."

The dollar value limitation of the warrant applies to the individual contract action, not to the underlying total contract value. For example, a contracting officer with a $10 million warrant can sign a $9 million modification to a $500 million contract. However, that same contracting officer cannot sign a new contract for $500 million.

Should you keep track of the warrant limitations of different contracting officers?

You should know the specific limitations set by the warrants of each contracting officer you encounter. Respectfully request a copy of these warrants from each contracting officer you deal with. You can also ask the chief of the contracting office for a list of all the warrants or for copies of the warrants.

Can any person other than the contracting officer make valid changes to my government contract?

No! Any changes or additions to your contract must go through the contracting officer. Be skeptical about any promises made or any assurances offered by any federal employee other than the contracting officer. Remember this adage: "Nothing is real until it comes from the contracting officer." If you find yourself negotiating with someone other than the contracting officer, you may be wasting your time. So, always involve the contracting officer.

How important is your relationship with the contracting officer?

Your goal is to have a positive and professional relationship with the contracting officer, who holds a great deal of power over your future. When you need that modification in 10 days or fewer, you should hope that the contracting officer knows your name. Five minutes of your time in a phone call may later save you or cost you millions of dollars. Every phone call or in-person meeting is worth hundreds of emails. Be always friendly and respectful.

Who is the contracting officer's representative or COR?

Contracting officers stay busy. They may sign hundreds or thousands of contracts over their careers. So, contracting officers cannot possibly administer every detail of every contract. Therefore, they delegate some of the administration to federal employees called *contracting officer's representatives* or *CORs*.

Who appoints the COR?

CORs are appointed by contracting officers, in writing, using a letter of designation. This letter describes the specific COR duties and responsibilities, identifies any limitations, and specifies the applicable period and extent of the COR's authority to act on behalf of the contracting officer. If you frequently work with a COR, you should request a copy of the designation letter of that COR, signed by the respective contracting officer.

Who is the program manager?

Program managers have authority over the entire portfolio, project, or program that your contract may support. Program managers do not have contractual authority, but they do have power over the direction and continuation of the program. You need to keep the program manager happy. You must remember that when the program manager gives you some direction that changes your contractual rights, you must notify the contracting officer to make official changes in writing to your contract.

Who is more important — the contracting officer or the program manager?

It depends. Sometimes the contracting officer is more powerful and can ruin your relationship with the client. Sometimes the program manager really calls the shots, and the contracting officer is merely an administrative clerk. You need to investigate your clients, get to know them, tread lightly, and determine how to navigate across conflicting priorities. Information, insights, or opinions about these dynamics are valuable.

Who is in the cast of characters for contractor companies?

Within companies, we will examine four roles that are important to the contract and its negotiation: contracts, legal, executives, and outside consultants.

Who is the company's contracts expert?

Much like the government side, most contractor companies have a single person responsible for contract negotiation and signature. This person may have very different titles, with many more possibilities than the standard *contracting officer* or *contract specialist* found in the government.

At contractor companies, you will probably encounter someone with one of these titles: contracts manager, director of contracts, or vice president of contracts. In smaller or more streamlined companies, the chief executive officer (CEO), chief financial officer (CFO), or chief operations officer (COO) may be responsible for contract negotiation and signature.

Who is the company's subcontracts expert?

Companies that have many subcontracts may designate a subcontracts manager who is responsible for the entire portfolio of subcontracts. Although the director of contracts focuses on all company contracts, the subcontracts manager deals with subcontracts exclusively.

Do some companies have multiple contracts and subcontracts managers?

Yes, some companies have so many contracts or subcontracts that they designate managers for a particular class, type, subset, or business line of contracts. For example, maybe the company has separate contracts managers for professional services, for information technology, for defense, and for intelligence contracts. If the company has a diverse portfolio of subcontracts, that company may have several subcontracts managers, each devoted to a subset of subcontracts.

Some companies split their contracts department into commercial and government sections. The commercial section focuses on business-to-business (B2B) contracts that do not involve federal clients, while the government section manages prime federal contracts and their related subcontracts. The rules of government contracting are different and complex, so sometimes this division makes sense.

Who is the company's legal expert?

In some companies, the general counsel or highest ranking attorney is responsible for negotiation and signature. Sometimes the general counsel is not directly responsible, but instead provides guidance, help, and final approval for contract negotiations performed by other company employees.

You may have heard the term *outside counsel*, which refers to the attorneys who represent the company, but do not work as full-time company employees. For example, the general counsel may hire several attorneys from an outside law firm to help with a lawsuit. The attorneys who work for the outside law firm, rather than the company, are called *outside counsel*.

What types of executives will you encounter during contract negotiation?

If your negotiation reaches a stalemate or encounters a difficult problem, maybe senior leadership will join the contracting process. It is not unusual for a president, vice president, or executive officer to participate in contract negotiation, especially if a disagreement cannot be resolved or it requires some special permission.

Will outside consultants become involved in contract negotiation?

Yes, possibly. Many companies hire www.ChristophLLC.com to assist with their government contract and subcontract negotiation. Do not be surprised if you encounter an outside consultant during your contract negotiation. If you need my help, email Christoph@ChristophLLC.com. You definitely want me on your side, rather than helping out your competitor!

CHAPTER 12, WHO SIGNS THE CONTRACT?

Who has the authority to sign contracts on behalf of the federal government?

Contracting officers! Also, the head of a federal agency has an inherent power to sign contracts on behalf of the agency, but agency heads usually delegate this power to the contracting officers.

Most contracts require two signatures: one by the contracting officer, and one on behalf of the contractor. Who signs first?

The contracting officer normally signs the contract only after it has been signed by the contractor. Usually, the contractor signs first, but sometimes the sequence is reversed.

Who should sign contracts on behalf of my company?

Your corporate policy should limit or define the officers who can sign government contracts. Some companies have internal policies that assign signature authority by job title or perhaps the dollar value or nature of the contract. Depending on the size of your company, you may assign one person the exclusive duty of signing government contracts and subcontracts. In the smallest companies, a lean leadership structure means the owner, CEO, or president signs the contracts.

Should I sign my legal name, or the company's legal name?

Remember that your contract with the government is with your company, not personally with you. For that reason, you should type the name of your company (because you are signing on behalf of the company). Then you should type your name and your job title as it relates to the company. For example, you could sign your name above this text:

Acme Manufacturing North America, LLC
Cornelius Stark, Managing Member

If you run a sole proprietorship or if you will sign the contract as an individual, then maybe you sign and type only your name. However, be careful. First consider forming a company (corporation, limited liability company, etc.) rather than operating as an individual or sole proprietorship. Of course, you should consult a business attorney and tax professional while making these decisions.

Chapter 13, Definitions, Ambiguities, Examples, and the Oxford Comma

Why should your contracts be written in plain English?

Writing your contracts in plain English makes everything easier. The contract is easier to read, understand, perform, and monitor. You will have fewer disagreements with clients with a contract written in simple language.

Use plain English! Avoid jargon. Do not use fancy language like "hereby" or "aforementioned." Do not use Latin words or any modern foreign language vocabulary if you can use plain English. Write shorter sentences, use simpler words, and break down complex ideas into separate paragraphs or sections.

Do first impressions matter when writing or editing contracts?

Yes, trust your first impression. If you cannot understand the contract, probably nobody else can understand it. If you think some language is unclear, clarify that language. If you find a badly disorganized section, streamline that section. If you find an awkwardly written sentence, rewrite it. Your goal is a contract written so clearly that everyone understands each section of it at first glance.

Why should you include a definitions section in your contract?

The *definitions section* ensures that all words, terms, and jargon will be understood in the same way by all parties to the contract. Definitions sections avoid ambiguities and disagreements. Always include a definitions section and include any words or terms that are not immediately obvious or that have multiple interpretations.

What if the word or term is not defined in the contract?

You should include specific guidance in your contract for this situation. You can follow the guidance from FAR Part 1, which states: "Undefined words retain their common dictionary meaning." But that convention may not settle the matter with finality. It may raise another question, such as…

Which "common dictionary" should my contract rely upon for undefined words?

Your contract should state what dictionary both parties will use to define any word or term not defined in the FAR, the solicitation, or the contract. Just pick one!

The decision to settle on a single dictionary will avoid disagreements, extensive research, and conflicting definitions from slightly differing dictionaries. Whether you prefer Merriam-Webster, Collins, Oxford, or American Heritage, make sure your contract states clearly which dictionary applies.

Why must you never repeat the same section twice in a contract?

Do not repeat the same thing. State it just once, and only once. Get it right the first time! Repetition will not help you. In fact, returning to the same topic or concept generates danger. Two or more statements of the same concept introduce the possibility of two or more interpretations. Differing interpretations of the same concept are disasters for contracts. They invite disagreements and lawsuits.

What is an ambiguity?

Ambiguity refers to when there are two or more reasonable interpretations of the same term or concept. Ambiguity is the sworn enemy of the scrivener (*scrivener* is an ancient word for a contract-drafter). One goal of writing a contract is to forge a single, mutual understanding of all the terms and conditions. Having multiple, reasonable interpretations defeats the purpose of the contract. Avoid ambiguities by never repeating concepts and always including a definitions section.

Are examples helpful in contracts?

Yes, including examples may avoid misunderstandings or misinterpretations. By using examples, the reader is assured of how formulas, processes, or concepts actually work. If you think it is helpful, include an example or two to clarify complex ideas. Your examples should use numbers, amounts, or events you may encounter in real life, rather than abstract or fantastical examples.

Why should you always use the Oxford comma in contracts?

The *Oxford comma* (also called the *serial comma*) refers to the comma following the second-to-last word in a list. By using the Oxford comma, you avoid misinterpretation and disagreement.

This sentence uses the Oxford comma: *The chef chopped the onions, garlic, and peppers.* This sentence omits the Oxford comma: *The chef chopped the onions, garlic and peppers.*

Always use the Oxford comma in contracts. The Oxford comma shows that the last two words or items in the list are separate and distinct. Let me explain with a colorful example.

Using the Oxford comma: *My parents, Tom Cruise, and Celine Dion attended the party.*
Omitting the Oxford comma: *My parents, Tom Cruise and Celine Dion attended the party.*

Do you see the ambiguity when you omit the Oxford comma? You could interpret the words to make Tom Cruise and Celine Dion into my parents, rather than two other party attendees. Nobody seeing the Oxford comma can make that mistake. Let me show you an example relevant to government contracts.

Using the Oxford comma: *The contractor shall deliver the mainframe components, wires, and batteries.* Omitting the Oxford comma: *The contractor shall deliver the mainframe components, wires and batteries.*

Do you see the ambiguity without the Oxford comma? You could interpret that the wires and batteries are included within the mainframe components, rather than existing as separate items for delivery.

Using the Oxford comma, it is clear that the contractor shall deliver three separate items: mainframe components, wires, and batteries. Use the Oxford comma in contracting documents!

CHAPTER 14, GETTING PAID: INVOICE AND PAYMENT TERMS

Why are payment clauses so important?

Your company needs to be paid on time in full. Cash flow is the lifeblood of business. Pay special attention to your payment clauses. Your contract with the government will not have much flexibility regarding payment clauses, but you should take special note of the payment terms. Your payment terms from the government should necessarily define the payment terms you negotiate with your subcontractors. You want to avoid the responsibility of paying subcontractors before your own company gets paid.

When you negotiate a contract or subcontract with another company, you have the greatest amount of flexibility in payment terms. Be extremely careful about the details of payment clauses.

You need to know *if* you will be paid and *when* you will be paid. Keep payment terms simple and clear to avoid confusion and delays.

What is a "pay when paid" term, condition, or clause?

Avoid contracts that state something like "We will pay you when we get paid." This arrangement can be a disaster for your company.

As a subcontractor, you can be several payment transactions separated from the government, who begins the cycle by paying the prime contractor first. If the government is 90 days late, the prime contractor will not pay your company for at least 90 days. Delays can get much worse if your company is a lower tier subcontractor, buried beneath several tiers of other subcontractors also waiting to get paid. You must avoid *pay when paid* contract terms.

Explain to your negotiation partner that the contract is between your two companies. If the government or any other company breaks its promises or fails to pay, that should not affect the contractual relationship between your two companies. Do not let your negotiation partner mix your company's interests with the potential failures of other parties. Do not let other people's problems become yours too. Keep the negotiation about payment terms between your company and the negotiation partner.

Why should I focus on days rather than contingencies?

Focus your payment schedules on days not contingencies. A contingency is a future event that is possible but cannot be predicted with certainty and may not even happen. You do not want your payments to be contingent; you want certain payments. Therefore, focus your payment terms on dates.

A contingent payment is something like "Contractor to be paid *if* the invoice is approved" or "Contractor will be paid *if* services are provided in a manner acceptable to buyer." The use of the word "if" in these examples signals the contingency. You want certainty, so you should remove any "if" or contingency. Do not give your negotiation partner the right to avoid payments because the partner might use that power not to pay you!

What are standard timelines for payment terms?

In government contracting, the timelines for payment can vary significantly. In my experience, payment terms of "Net 30" and "Net 15" for small businesses are common, although some contracts have lengthy timelines of 60 or even 90 days until payment.

What does "Net 30" or "Net 15" mean for payment terms?

"Net 30" means the buyer must pay within 30 days after receipt of the invoice. "Net 15" means payment arrives within 15 days after the invoice.

The smaller your business, the more likely your negotiating partner may accommodate "Net 15" instead of "Net 30." The federal government — and as a consequence, federal contractors and subcontractors — are incentivized and sometimes required to accelerate payments to small business subcontractors. Therefore, government contracting policy encourages faster payment to small businesses by using a "Net 15" schedule.

What does "2% 10, Net 30" mean for payment terms?

Some companies will provide a discount for early payment. "2% 10, Net 30" means that if you pay the invoice within 10 days, you receive a 2% discount. If the invoice is for $1,000, the required payment is only $980 if paid within 10 days. The $1,000 is due within 30 days, but within 10 days, only $980 is due, after the 2% discount.

Sometimes these discounts for early payment are written in different ways, such as "2/10, Net 30" or "2-10 Net 30" or by other formulas. Just remember to separate the "Net 30" from the discount terms. The discount terms include two numbers—the discount as a percentage and the number of days from invoice to trigger the discount. Therefore, we can translate the following examples:

"5/10, Net 30" means a discount of 5% if paid within 10 days.
"2%-15, Net 30" means a discount of 2% if paid within 15 days.
"5/5, Net 30" means a discount of 5% if paid within 5 days.

Now you understand the pattern!

Why should I pay attention to any review or approval process for invoices?

The details of your negotiation partner's process for reviewing or approving invoices may significantly delay your payment. You may expect the invoice to be approved instantly or it may not even need any approval to be paid, but the other company may have a payment process that takes days or weeks.

Negotiate away the risks of delayed payment by stating that "Net 15" means payment is due 15 days after the invoice is received regardless of any internal review or approval procedures. Remember, one goal of your contract is to achieve certainty and timeliness for payment! Cash flow is the lifeblood of any business, so avoid "blood clots and heart attacks!"

How should I structure late payment fees?

You should consider including late payment fees. Otherwise, your negotiation partner has less incentive to pay on time. If you choose to include late payment fees, make them simple and easy to calculate.

Many late payment fees require the payment of interest in addition to the outstanding (late) payment. Make sure you explain how this interest is calculated.

Other late payment fees use a lump-sum penalty. For example, $500 for every week the payment is past due.

Whether you structure late payment fees based on interest rates or lump-sum amounts, be careful about any legal (statutory) limitations. Contact an attorney to determine if your relevant jurisdiction forbids any late payment fees beyond a certain amount or rate. For example, to protect homeowners, many American states passed laws limiting the amount of late payment fees for mortgage payments. Similar limitations may apply to your contract for products or services.

How should I structure lump-sum payment fees?

The lump sum should be a small fraction of the actual payment owed. Decide on a length of time whereby the lump sum will be applied again to the outstanding amount owed. For example, $100 in late fees applied every month the payment is overdue.

What is the difference between liquidated damages and late payment fees?

You may have heard of the term *liquidated damages*, which are paid on a daily or weekly basis when the schedule of a project falls behind. Construction contracts often use liquidated damages. For example, the builder pays liquidated damages of $1 million for every week beyond the scheduled completion date in the contract.

Are liquidated damages considered penalties?

While liquidated damages are similar to late payment fees, you should know they are different. Liquidated damages are not and cannot be penalties. Instead, liquidated damages are designed to compensate the injured party for the damages of the slipped schedule or late delivery.

Liquidated damages are a shortcut to proving "damages" (monetary compensation) if the contract is broken or one party fails to deliver or perform. Instead of requiring a lawsuit to prove those monetary damages, a liquidated damages provision estimates those monetary damages within the contract and requires one party to pay them in the event of default or failure to deliver or perform. In this way, liquidated damages protect against risk and avoid the cost and uncertainty of litigation. Liquidated damages can be ruled as unenforceable if the amount is so high that a court considers it a penalty. Therefore, liquidated damages cannot be penalties.

Should you describe late payment fees as penalties?

No, call them *late payment fees*, not penalties. Although the late payment fee — in plain English — seems like a penalty, you should not call it a "penalty." You do not want the late payment fees to be ruled as unenforceable.

When should you use late payment fees versus liquidated damages?

In most cases, you can easily negotiate late payment fees. Leave the liquidated damages terms for complex contracts for very large amounts of money where failures or delays create serious problems for one or both parties. Otherwise, liquidated damages may not be worth the hassle of calculation and negotiation because late payment fees are simpler and easier to establish.

How should I structure the interest rate of late payment fees?

The simplest method is to choose a fixed interest rate that does not change, such as 1% or 5%. A more complicated method is to tie the interest rate to the Consumer Price Index or some other publicly available data point. I recommend that you choose a fixed interest rate.

What is the difference between simple interest and compound interest?

State whether the interest will accrue based on *simple interest* or *compound interest*. While *simple interest* is based only on the original principal (the outstanding payment), *compound interest* will slowly add the late payment fees to the principal (the outstanding payment).

These mathematical rules make a big difference over time. Pull out a calculator and see the difference in the example of a 1% late payment fee for $1,000,000 based on *simple interest* versus *compound interest* for one year, compounded monthly.

What is a grace period?

Grace periods seem silly. Although payment is due on the first of the month, the payer has a 10-day grace period. Pause and think. Is the payment *really* due on the first of the month if there is a 10-day grace period? Not really.

A grace period is an amount of time beyond the due date that does not trigger any late payment fees. In my opinion, grace periods are not useful to a small business contractor expecting payment on time.

Should I include a grace period for late payments?

The decision to include a grace period invites debate. Personally, I see no merit in grace periods. You negotiate a contract to structure definite payments at specific points in time. Why promote any "wiggle room" that confuses the calculation of late payment fees? I prefer a firm, fixed date for payment with no grace period. Why should you confuse the certainty of the due date and late fees by adding a grace period?

CHAPTER 15, HOW TO ASK FOR MORE MONEY: REAS VERSUS CLAIMS

If circumstances change, are you entitled to more money for your government contract?

Perhaps. Maybe. "It depends!"

You need to know how to ask for more money on your government contract. The goal is to get a modification that gives you more money than you originally negotiated. Two separate but similar methods allow you to ask for more money: (1) submit a *request for equitable adjustment* (REA) or (2) file a *claim*. Start with the REA, because you can charge the government for your preparation costs, such as hiring a consultant to help you. If the REA is denied, then you can submit a *claim*, which requires the government to respond in writing within a certain time. If the contracting officer denies your claim, you can appeal the claim in federal court or at the boards of contract appeals.

Why should you organize your reasons for asking for more money?

Before you ask for more money, you need to determine whether you are entitled to more money. You must specify a legitimate reason, not just a sad story about costs that have increased. The first step is to decide which clause in your contract entitles you to more money. The most common clause to be cited is some form of the Changes clause, which authorizes the government to make changes within the scope of the contract.

Does the Changes clause require the government to pay for the added costs of any change orders?

Yes! The Changes clause allows the government to make unilateral changes to certain parts of the contract, and you must comply if the Changes clause is in your contract. That was part of the deal that you negotiated and signed. If these changes cost money, then the government must pay you.

What is the request for more money called?

Your written request for money due to changes in the contract is called a *request for equitable adjustment* or REA. Another form of a written request for money is called a *claim*. The REA requires a special format and specific certifications to be valid. Like the REA, the claim also requires a special format and specific certifications to be valid.

What is the difference between a claim and REA?

The difference between a claim and REA is complex. Get a free copy of my full-length article on this topic by emailing Christoph@ChristophLLC.com.

What are the basic differences between a claim and REA?

Here are the basics. REAs and claims are two methods for asking for more money for your government contracts. Although REAs and claims are similar, they differ significantly. The biggest differences appear during the processes after you submit your REA or claim.

Is the REA considered contract administration or litigation?

REAs are considered contract administration rather than litigation. When you submit the REA, you are not taking the first step in suing the government. REAs are not lawsuits. They are merely a normal part of government contract administration. Contract administration costs can be paid by the government. For this reason, you can bill the government for the costs of preparing your REA.

Can the REA request the payment of preparation costs in the total amount?

Yes. If you hire a consultant like www.ChristophLLC.com to help you prepare the REA, you can include your consultant costs as preparation costs in the total amount requested by the REA. In fact, Christoph LLC has successfully written several REAs that got my clients paid, in full, including the Christoph LLC consulting bills. My clients were fully reimbursed by the government for the costs of hiring Christoph LLC for work on the REA, as well as for the underlying basis of the original REA. This tremendous advantage of the REA demonstrates why you should try the REA before the claim.

Does the REA create a deadline for the government to respond?

Unfortunately, no deadline applies for the government to respond to your REA. The government can ignore your REA indefinitely. The government could stall, postpone, and delay your REA for months or years. For this reason, you should set firm deadlines for when the government must respond. If you get no response by the deadline, either forward the REA to higher level government officials, or choose to submit a claim instead.

Does the certified claim under the Contract Disputes Act create a deadline for the government to respond?

Yes, the claim starts a deadline that requires a written response from the government, but the REA does not. Unlike REAs, claims force the government contracting officer to respond within a certain period of time. Therefore, a certified claim under the Contract Disputes Act is considered more aggressive than a REA.

Is a claim the first step toward a formal process of litigation?

Yes. Claims, unless negotiated and settled, form the basis of adversarial litigation between the government and your company. To encourage settlement, all claims must start with the contracting officer. Certified claims under the Contract Disputes Act are the first step toward formal litigation, but they must first give the contracting officer a chance to settle the claim.

How must the contracting officer respond to a certified claim?

After receiving the claim, the contracting officer must issue your company a Final Decision. The Final Decision approves or denies your claim and provides reasoning.

Can you appeal the Final Decision of your claim?

Yes. Once your company receives the Final Decision, you have the option to appeal to either the boards of contract appeals or the United States Court of Federal Claims. In either venue, you can further appeal to the United States Court of Appeals for the Federal Circuit and then to the Supreme Court of the United States.

Can you skip the contracting officer and take your claim directly to court?

No, you cannot take your claim directly to court. First, you must submit the claim to the contracting officer and receive the Final Decision. Again, this submission encourages settlement without litigation. You want to get more money for your government contract, and you do not want to spend more money on an expensive lawsuit.

Does the REA, rather than the claim, involve courts or litigation?

No, REAs do not involve courts or lawsuits. Ideally, your REA will be resolved quickly and amicably between your company and the contracting officer. Your REA can be resolved by a friendly discussion over the phone that is formalized in a modification to the government contract. Your claim, on the other hand, could turn into a contentious, expensive, and time-consuming legal battle.

What are the certification requirements for the claim versus the REA?

Claims and REAs have different certification requirements. The confusing factor is that both require two identical certifications, but the claim alone also requires two other additional certifications. This distinction means that REAs must contain two written certifications, while claims require four written certifications.

Are the required certifications "magic words" or can you change them as you prefer?

These certifications should be considered magic words. Do not alter the certifications or get creative. These words ensure that your REA or your claim will be legitimate and not be rejected. Even more importantly, if you forget the magic words in the four certifications for your claim, then no clock has started ticking. Your claim was in fact "defective." Forgetting the four certifications means your claim never really occurred and the contracting officer is under no deadline to respond and provide your company a Final Decision for the claim. When your company submits a claim or REA, you must make sure you have an expert in government contracting to assist.

What is a concise summary of the differences between the claim versus the REA?

Request for equitable adjustment or REA:

>Considered contract administration.
>You can include preparation costs.
>Not litigation and not the start of a lawsuit.
>Less formal and less aggressive than a claim.
>No timeline for the contracting officer to respond.

Claim under the Contract Disputes Act:

>Considered litigation.
>You cannot include preparation costs.
>Starts with the contracting officer.
>Can result in a lawsuit.
>More formal and more aggressive than an REA.
>Strict time limits for the contracting officer to respond.

CHAPTER 16, NEGOTIATING MODIFICATIONS AND CHANGE ORDERS

What is a modification?

A *modification* is a formal, written change to your contract.

Regarding modifications, what is the most important power to reserve?

Make sure your contracts can be modified only by written changes that are signed by both parties. When negotiating a subcontract between two companies, you must reserve the power to modify the contract on a bilateral basis (after both parties sign the modification). Do not grant your negotiation partner the ability to make unilateral, one-sided changes to the contract.

What types of changes can a modification effect in my contract?

Modifications can create a wide variety of changes, including price increases or decreases, schedule extensions or accelerations, or the removal or addition of clauses. A contract modification can change the *Statement of Work* or specifications you follow to deliver the products or provide the services.

Whatever types of change the modification creates, you must identify and understand every single change. Never sign a modification that contains changes you do not understand. Just like the folk adage to "Look before you leap," you must thoroughly investigate every modification before you agree to its terms by signing your name. If you need help understanding what your modifications actually mean, send me an email at Christoph@ChristophLLC.com.

Why is it important to carefully limit your negotiation partner's ability to terminate or change the contract without your approval?

Some companies will try to sneak in the power to unilaterally terminate the contract simply because the government holds this power over the prime contractor (using the *Termination for Convenience clause*). In turn, the prime contractor believes it must hold this power over the subcontractor.

This fear is valid because if the prime contractor is terminated, it needs a way to terminate its subcontractors. If the prime contractor is no longer paid to continue the work, it does not want to pay its subcontractors to continue the terminated work. Therefore, prime contractors need to *flow down* the government's power to terminate some or all of the contract.

Similarly, many prime contracts contain the *Changes clause*, which allows the government to make unilateral changes within certain parameters. If the government unilaterally changes the requirements or specifications of the prime contract, the prime contractor needs its subcontractors to adopt the same changes. Therefore, prime contractors face significant risk if they do not *flow down* the government's power to change the prime contract.

How should you protect your company while mitigating the prime contractor's risk?

Use this simple solution to eliminate the prime contractor's risk while protecting your company from unnecessary or unwanted changes. In your subcontract, allow the prime contractor to change or terminate the subcontract *only if the government initiates* such a change or termination. Require written proof that the government changed or terminated the prime contract for this subcontract provision to take effect.

You should also narrow the prime contractor's opportunity by limiting the change or termination to the minimum amount necessary to comply with the government's modification. For example, if the government terminates a fraction of the work that was to be performed by the subcontractor, the prime contractor can terminate only that fraction, not the entire project. Craft language that limits the prime contractor's ability to *unilaterally* change or terminate your subcontract only to the extent necessary. Require written proof of the government's change or termination. By following these guidelines, you eliminate the risk to the prime contractor while protecting your company from being treated unfairly.

What is a unilateral modification?

A *unilateral modification* changes the terms and conditions of your contract but requires no signature. Therefore, the modification is issued *unilaterally*.

Can the government change my prime contract without my permission?

Yes. Most government contracts contain some version of the *Changes clause*, which allows the government to make unilateral modifications without your permission. In effect, you already agreed to these future modifications by signing the original contract that included the Changes clause.

What is a bilateral modification?

A *bilateral modification* changes the terms and conditions of your contract using a signature from both the contracting officer and contractor. Another term for bilateral modification is *supplemental agreement*.

What is an administrative change or administrative modification?

An *administrative change* or *administrative modification* is a type of unilateral modification that does not affect the rights or obligations of the contractor. For example, the contracting officer may change the type of appropriated money used to pay you, or may change the government payment office that sends you money, but there is no effect on your payments or rights.

Can a unilateral modification change my obligations under the contract?

Yes, for example, a unilateral modification under the *Changes clause* requires your company to comply. Although your company may be entitled to an *equitable adjustment* (more money), you are obligated to follow the directions of any proper exercise of the Changes clause. Another example is a unilateral *exercise of an option*: Your company has no choice but to perform the option period if it is properly exercised in a unilateral modification.

How can I distinguish between unilateral and bilateral modifications?

Always look at Block 13 of the *Standard Form (SF) 30*, which describes the contracting officer's authority or justification for issuing the modification.

What is the Changes clause?

Several versions of the *Changes clause* allow the government to change the contract unilaterally, within certain limits, using a change order. Your company must comply with authorized changes, although you may be entitled to an *equitable adjustment*.

What is a change order?

A *change order* is any form of written direction from the contracting officer that requires your company to perform the contract differently. The change order can be a formal modification or an email or a letter. Based on the *Changes clause*, the contracting officer directs some change and your company must comply. However, your company may be entitled to an *equitable adjustment* (more money, a schedule extension, or some other relief).

Do commercial government contracts allow for unilateral change orders?

No, commercial government contracts using FAR Part 12 procedures do not allow for unilateral changes. All changes under commercial government contracts must be agreed upon by signature of the contracting officer and contractor. If your commercial government contract includes some version of the Changes clause, you should negotiate to remove it.

What is a constructive change?

A *constructive change* is a doctrine of law invented by judges that protects your company from getting "ripped off." If the contracting officer's words, writings, communications, acts, or failure to act causes your company to make changes under the contract—even though there was no formal change order—the *doctrine of constructive changes* may entitle your company to an equitable adjustment. In other words, if the contracting officer's action or inaction seems like a change order—even though it was not a formal, written change order—it may be construed or interpreted as if it were a formal, written change order.

This doctrine protects your company from being swindled by a contracting officer who nudges you towards different work and refuses to pay you because "there was no official, written change order." Be careful about relying on constructive changes. A better idea is to ask for a written modification whenever you suspect a change order or any change to the contract.

What is an equitable adjustment?

An *equitable adjustment* is a modification to the contract price, schedule, or other terms to reflect changed circumstances. Most equitable adjustments are in response to a change order directed by the contracting officer under the Changes clause. For example:

1. Contracting officer issues a change order to use more expensive material.
2. Your company complies with the change order because of the Changes clause.
3. Your company incurs greater costs than contemplated under the original contract.

4. Your company submits a request for equitable adjustment (REA) for more money.
5. Contracting officer grants your REA.
6. Contracting officer modifies the contract to pay you more money (equitable adjustment).

What is a request for equitable adjustment or REA?

Learn more about *requests for equitable adjustment (REA)* and *claims* under the Contract Disputes Act in the chapter, "How to Ask for More Money: REA versus Claims." You can also read my full-length article on this topic by emailing me at Christoph@ChristophLLC.com.

If a modification is described as "no big deal," why should my company take a closer look?

Sometimes the government contracting officer will include changes or updates to clauses in the contract. "No big deal," the contracting officer may say. "These are just the latest versions of the same clauses."

Do not fall for this dirty trick. Yes, of course, the Federal Acquisition Regulation (FAR) clauses change over time. Yes, it is true that each FAR clause shows the timing of the last update or version of that clause—for example, November 2016. None of this information is relevant to your specific contract. Your specific contract was a deal you struck, precisely showing all the clauses in your contract, as of the date of the contract.

If the government wants to change or update any of these clauses, your company may be entitled to receive more money or some other *consideration*. When you hear the term *consideration*, think of money or something else of recognizable value.

What is a Contractor's Statement of Release?

Sometimes the modification will include language that waives your right to request money or other relief to comply with the new clauses. Watch out for this language in your modification:

> "Contractor's Statement of Release
> In consideration of the modification(s) agreed to herein as complete equitable adjustments for the Contractor's _____ (describe) _____ "proposal(s) for adjustment," the Contractor hereby releases the Government from any and all liability under this contract for further equitable adjustments attributable to such facts or circumstances giving rise to the "proposal(s) for adjustment" (except for_____)."

You might sign this modification, eager to proceed, but not recognizing that you are also signing away your rights to additional money. Do not make this mistake. Review every modification carefully, even if it's "no big deal."

Should you permit any changes to the contract that are not formalized in writing?

No. Do not allow anyone (the government, your prime contractor, your subcontractor) to make changes to your business relationship that are not established in writing. The change can start off with a conversation, but it must be followed by something in writing. I have seen so many disasters that could have been avoided by following this advice. Formalize all changes in writing within the contract!

Chapter 17, Negotiating Option Periods

What is an option period in the context of government contracting?

Most government contracts are for a total of 5 years. The 5 years are usually separated into 1-year periods of performance. The first year is the *base period* and starts shortly after you sign the contract. The next 4 years are *option periods*. When you signed the contract, your company also agreed to the possibility of performing the option periods.

The government gets your company to continue performance through the option periods by *exercising* an option. If the government does not exercise the next option period, your contractual obligations to perform are finished.

What does it mean to exercise an option?

Exercise an option is a fancy term for when the government orders your company to perform an option. Some people describe it as "activating" the option period or "turning on" the option CLIN (contract line item number). Your company will receive a written modification to the contract which exercises the option period.

Is the government required to exercise any option under my contract?

No, because if the government were somehow required to exercise an option, then it would be an obligation, not an option. The government has the *unilateral right* to exercise any option.

Can you negotiate option periods?

Your opportunity to negotiate changes to the option period comes before signing the contract. After you sign the contract and agree to the option terms, the options are a unilateral right of the government. By definition, option periods give the government the sole discretion to exercise or not exercise each option period. The contractor has no control over whether the option periods will be performed because the decision remains with the government client.

What do you mean by unilateral right?

The government's right to exercise the option is *unilateral* because your company cannot reject the exercised option. Your company does not need to sign or agree to anything. The government sends you a written modification that exercises the option, and your company is obligated to perform.

Can a contractor refuse to perform an option period?

No! If your company refuses to perform a properly exercised option, your company is failing to follow the terms of the contract you signed. When you fail to perform, you risk being *terminated for default*. As a federal contractor, a termination for default is effectively a "death sentence" for your business!

Will my company get advance notification before the government exercises the option?

Yes, the standard FAR clause for options requires the government to notify your company in writing of its intent to exercise the option.

How far in advance will my company be notified in writing?

Read the options clause in your contract. The advance notification timeline can be tailored or changed by the contracting officer, so you need to check your contract. Some contracting officers write in a notification timeline of 30 days before exercising the option. Others will notify your company 15 days in advance. I have seen many government contracts that require advance notice of only 1 day before, and even a few that allow *any time* before the option period of performance. For these reasons, you need to mark your calendar after you check your government contracts so that you will never be surprised by an option period. You should also mark your calendar so that if you fail to receive a notification of the intent to exercise the option, you can contact the government to determine if it happened by mistake or by design.

Are you saying the government sometimes forgets to exercise an option?

Yes, I am warning you the government sometimes forgets to exercise an option. Your company should keep good track of all the dates and contact the contracting officer immediately if you think you're missing a notification or option exercise. You may save yourself from losing a valuable contract and save the contracting officer from embarrassment and inconvenience.

What happens if the contracting officer forgets to exercise the option in time?

Options must be exercised in precisely the same way they were negotiated in the contract. If the contracting officer fails to follow any material condition, such as the notification requirement, the government loses the *unilateral right* to exercise the option. In other words, your company is no longer obligated to perform the option period.

Can my company "walk away" from the contract if the government fails to exercise the option properly?

Yes, if the government forgets or fails to exercise your option in time, your company has a choice. You can walk away, with no penalties. The government cannot force you to perform because it lost the *unilateral right* to exercise the option.

Instead, you can negotiate with the government to sign a *bilateral modification* (signed by your company and the government) that "re-creates" the option period to fix the mistake. Some contracting officers or government attorneys will say you cannot fix the mistake and you must solicit, compete, and sign an entirely new contract. Your company cannot do much about risk-averse government employees, but you could persistently request a modification to your current contract.

Is it a bad sign if the government does not exercise my option and that choice was not a mistake?

Yes, if the government purposefully declined to exercise your option, that choice is a very bad sign for your company. For some reason, the government does not want your company to perform the remaining periods of the contract.

Maybe you failed to satisfy the government. Maybe the government officials think they can get a better deal elsewhere. Maybe the government no longer needs the subject of the contract. In any case, your company loses future revenue.

Can the contracting officer update my FAR clauses when exercising the option?

Yes, but by changing the FAR clauses, the government loses its right to exercise the option unilaterally (without your permission). Your company agreed to perform the option period when it signed the contract, but your company did not agree to the updates to the FAR clause. The contracting officer must separate these modifications to retain the right to unilaterally exercise your option.

While the contracting officer can combine the option exercise with other changes, this combination means your company may be entitled to an "equitable adjustment," meaning money, schedule extensions, or other contractual relief.

Why should I investigate further if the contracting officer requests my signature when exercising an option?

Let's say your contracting officer sends your company a modification to exercise the next option period and requires your signature. This seems like welcome news. Your company receives new work and an extension of the period of performance. Your company gets 365 more days of revenue from this contract.

Be careful if the government requests your signature. Technically, there is no need for your company to countersign the option exercise. The government has the right to exercise the option unilaterally. That pattern is how options work. The government does not need your permission to exercise the option under standard FAR clauses, so the government may request your signature for you to accept other changes in the contract, such as updates to FAR clauses.

If your company does not need to countersign an option exercise modification, the government has no reason to ask for your signature (other than an innocent reason: to ensure your company realizes the option was exercised). This request for signature could mean your company is signing away its rights on several other issues.

Be careful. Make sure to read the details of the modification. The government might not tell you how the modification to exercise the option has some other important changes. Send a copy of the modification to your designated government contracting expert before you sign it. Make sure you review every modification, especially those described as "no big deal."

CHAPTER 18, NEGOTIATING THE STATEMENT OF WORK

What is the Statement of Work (SOW)?

The *Statement of Work* (SOW) contains the technical specifications or nitty-gritty details of what you must perform or deliver to satisfy the contract. While the rest of the contract may contain important details, the SOW clearly defines the work or specific activities. When your employees need to know if a particular task is required by the contract, the first place to look is the SOW.

How should you negotiate the SOW as a prime contractor?

If you are the prime contractor, the SOW is probably defined by the government, so you have little influence over the content of the SOW. However, when negotiating a subcontract, both parties have significant flexibility in fleshing out the details of the SOW.

As the prime contractor, ensure the SOW covers all responsibilities and duties that you expect the subcontractor to perform. If the subcontractor fails to perform, the prime contractor takes all the blame from the government. Write a thorough and comprehensive SOW that leaves nothing to chance. The prime contractor's incentive is to negotiate a broader and detailed SOW that requires more from the subcontractor. Convincing a subcontractor to perform something not explicitly written into the SOW is difficult and potentially costly. Prevent this possibility by thoroughly reviewing the SOW before signature.

How should you negotiate the SOW as a subcontractor?

As the subcontractor, or party that must perform the SOW, negotiate for reasonable performance standards. Make no promises you cannot keep. If you think the SOW is too strict, too comprehensive, too complicated, or impossible to perform, you need to negotiate changes before signing the contract. Do not be afraid to ask questions or challenge assumptions. The subcontractor's incentive is to negotiate a narrow SOW that clearly defines and limits the obligations of the subcontractor.

How can you limit the scope of a SOW?

Avoid open-ended promises, commitments, or requirements. Contract requirements must be clearly defined in terms of activities, rather than aspirational goals. Focus on measurable quantities, specific activities, and objective results.

Should the SOW exclude certain activities by defining them as "out of scope?"

Yes. Be specific about what is *not* included in the SOW. Identify services, products, tasks, or activities that are *not* within the scope of the contract. List those services, products, tasks, or activities that are outside of the scope of the contract, so that nobody can perceive that your company is responsible. For example, if the equipment is to be provided by the prime contractor, write that into the SOW so that fact is incorporated into the contract. Do not rely on previous conversations or assumptions.

Should you refer to any assumptions or contingencies that may affect the SOW?

Yes. Include any assumptions or contingencies that affect how and whether your company can perform the work. Write these assumptions or contingencies into the contract or SOW. For example, a lawn-mowing company cannot properly cut grass in rainy weather, nor can they mow grass that is blocked, covered, or inaccessible. Therefore, the savvy lawn-mowing company may include assumptions like favorable weather conditions and accessible lawns free of obstructions.

Why are there so many "shall" phrases or commands in the SOW?

The government really, *really* likes using the word "shall" in contracts. Rather than "must" or "need" or any other word, contracting officers prefer to use "shall" to issue commands or define requirements. For example, "The contractor shall provide help desk support seven days per week."

Perhaps "shall" became the favored term because that word is used throughout the FAR. Or maybe the word "shall" spread through many years of habit and practice. No matter the origination, you will find this word in your prime contracts and subcontracts. Following the government lead, prime contractors and subcontractors usually include the word "shall" in their contracts and subcontracts.

Can you use the word "must" instead of "shall" in the SOW?

I defer to the opinions of others on this topic of *must* versus *shall*. Common practice in government contracting is to use *shall*.

However, just because something *is* does not mean it *should be.* The philosopher David Hume describes the error of confusing what exists with what is ideal as the *is-ought problem.* But that topic is for another, different book!

Should the SOW contain a definitions section?

Yes, always include a definitions section in the SOW. By defining your terms, you will avoid misunderstandings and misinterpretations, which lead to conflicts and disagreements. Any word that is not immediately obvious — or that has multiple definitions or interpretations — should be carefully defined. When in doubt, define your terms!

Should the SOW be written in plain English?

Yes, write the SOW in plain English. Use fewer words. Use simpler words. Use shorter sentences. Avoid technical terms and jargon. If you must use technical terms or jargon, include them in a definitions sections.

Is active voice better than passive voice?

Use the active voice of verbs, not the passive voice. My advice applies to most writing, not just government contracts. Improve your writing. Favor the active voice.

Should you proofread the SOW?

Carefully proofread and edit the SOW for errors, clarity, style, grammar, and other improvements. Send the SOW to a colleague to get a second review. Your extra effort now may prevent painful problems in the future.

What is performance-based acquisition?

Performance-based acquisition uses a *Performance Work Statement (PWS)* instead of a Statement of Work (SOW), measurable performance standards, and a method of measuring contractor performance against these objective standards.

The goal of performance-based acquisition is to save money and achieve better results by using commercial solutions. Instead of telling the experts in industry how to perform services, ask for the desired outcome and let the contractor impress the client with its ingenuity.

What is the difference between a PWS and SOW?

A *Performance Work Statement (PWS)* describes measurable performance standards (quality, timeliness, quantity) and focuses on the desired outcome. In contrast, a *Statement of Work (SOW)* provides detailed instructions for how to perform the work.

For example, a SOW might state that "the contractor shall use a gas-powered lawn mower, three times per month, during daylight hours to mow the grass on the Army base." In contrast, a PWS might state that "the contractor shall keep the grass on the Army base between three and five inches in height at all times." The SOW dictates exactly how the contractor will cut the grass, while the PWS lets the contractor figure out the most sensible way to achieve the desired result.

This example PWS has measurable performance standards: the height of the grass should be always between three and five inches. In this example, the government's method of measuring the contractor's performance might be a "spot check" once per week with measuring tape.

Is the difference between a PWS and SOW sometimes illusory, and merely "form over substance?"

Yes, unfortunately. In the real world, sometimes the government employee literally deletes the title of "Statement of Work" and substitutes "Performance Work Statement," with no substantive differences whatsoever. This so-called "PWS" describes exactly how your company must perform the work, rather than describing the desired results. When this tomfoolery happens, we have a case of form over substance. The document has a new title (PWS) but nothing is changed. You may encounter a so-called "PWS" that is merely a SOW in disguise.

How does the government measure whether the contractor meets the performance standards of a PWS?

One common method for measuring the contractor's adherence to the performance standards of a PWS is called a *Quality Assurance Surveillance Plan* or *QASP* (rhymes with "wasp"). Sometimes the government designs the QASP and sometimes the government requires the contractor to design the QASP. Either way, the QASP will be a critical document to measure your success under the government contract. Become familiar with the QASP, which will describe exactly how and when the government will "checkup" on your performance.

CHAPTER 19, NEGOTIATING LABOR RATES AND WRAP RATES

What are the critical negotiation terms and concepts for anyone who charges by the hour?

If you sell your services by the hour, you need to understand labor rates, wrap rates, time and materials contracts, and labor-hour contracts. Most importantly, you must know how to calculate your fully loaded labor rate.

What if my negotiation partner requests a decrease to my standard rate?

You need to make this decision yourself. If you can maintain profitability at the lesser payment rate, maybe you should agree to the new contract term. But you may want to hold a firm stance on your minimum billing rate. Agreeing to discounts or lesser payment rates can be a slippery slope that leads to unprofitability and bankruptcy. Also consider that future clients may demand the same discounts if they hear "through the grapevine" that you are willing to lower your payment rates.

Some companies offer a standard rate that is discounted by volume. For example, if your standard rate is $100 per hour, you offer a discounted rate of $90 per hour for projects greater than 1,000 hours. The increased volume offsets the reduction in your hourly rate, and having a long-term client reduces the cost of searching for new clients.

What is a time and materials contract?

Time and materials government contracts are very similar to contracts you see for plumbers, attorneys, or car mechanics. You pay your attorney by the hour, and you pay for your attorney's costs, such as postage or court filing fees. You pay your plumber by the hour, and you pay for your plumber's costs, such as pipes, equipment, and new toilets.

When the government is the client, the government pays your company by the hour, and the government also pays for your materials used in the contract. Or in a subcontract between two companies, the prime contractor pays your company for hourly services and for the cost of materials. These are both examples of a *time and materials contract.*

What is a labor-hour contract?

Labor-hour contracts are a subset of time and materials contracts. Labor-hour contracts are basically the same, except they involve no materials.

The government or prime contractor pays your company only by the hour, for labor. No materials exist in a labor-hour contract. For example, your labor-hour contract pays your company an hourly rate for every hour of work your employee completes onsite at the government building.

What is a fully loaded labor rate?

The *fully loaded labor rate* is the rate you bill your clients. When you win a time and materials or labor-hour contract, you need to decide how much to bill the client per hour of work. This rate must be higher than the direct labor rate your company pays the employee. Otherwise, how can you generate a profit?

If you win a government contract based on time and materials, the "time" will be measured in labor hours. Your company will be paid for each hour of work and for any materials used. Each hour of work will be classified according to a labor category and labor rate. Your experienced employees will have a more expensive labor rate because they cost you more to employ. Your less experienced employees will have a cheaper labor rate.

Can you provide an example of calculating the fully loaded labor rate?

If your company pays one employee $50 per hour, you need to bill that employee's labor hours at a higher labor rate, otherwise your company will not make a profit. Start with the $50 per hour (direct cost), then apply the indirect costs of that employee and add profit for your company. Let's say your indirect costs per labor hour is $10. Your profit per labor hour is $5. Now you have a fully loaded labor rate:

Direct labor rate (what you pay the employee) + indirect costs + profit = fully loaded labor rate

$50 + $10 + $5 = $65

Mathematically restated, this equation transforms into:

Fully loaded labor rate – indirect costs – profit = direct labor rate your company pays the employee

$65 – $10 – $5 = $50

See how it all adds up?

The fully loaded labor rate captures the individual, direct, hourly labor rate for a particular labor category, along with the indirect costs and profit for your company. In time and materials contracts, you must always bill your labor rates as fully loaded labor rates. Otherwise, you will shortchange your company.

What happens if you fail to bill the fully loaded labor rate?

Following the earlier example, if you billed your employee at $50 per hour on a time and materials contract, this would be a rookie mistake. You forgot to add the indirect costs and your company profit. Your client compensates you for the direct cost of the employee but not for any of the indirect costs.

Why is it so important to bill the fully loaded labor rate in time and materials or labor-hour contracts?

If you fail to bill for the fully loaded rate, you will fail to earn a sustainable profit. You must propose, quote, bill, and charge fully loaded labor rates in your time and materials contracts. Make sure the fully loaded labor rate captures all costs for that employee's labor category: direct costs, indirect costs, fringe benefits like healthcare, etc. Of course, you must not forget profit! Your company needs a government contracting expert or accountant to help you with these cost calculations.

What is a wrap rate?

The *wrap rate* is the multiplier your company uses to transform the employee's direct, hourly cost into a fully loaded labor rate. In the earlier example, the wrap rate is calculated by dividing the fully loaded labor rate by the direct cost of $50 per hour.

Wrap rate = fully loaded labor rate / direct labor rate

1.3 = $65 / $50

$65 is 130% of $50

In this example, the wrap rate or wrap multiplier is 1.3 or 130%. The fully loaded labor rate is 130% of the direct labor rate your company pays the employee. If you multiply the direct labor rate by 1.3, you arrive at the fully loaded labor rate.

Can you negotiate your company's wrap rate?

Not really. Your company, not your negotiation partner, controls the wrap rate by changing direct and indirect costs. Your negotiation partner may want you to have a lower wrap rate to be competitive for a particular contracting opportunity, but your company needs to change something to achieve a different wrap rate. Your competitor cannot change your wrap rate because the wrap rate is a function of your company costs.

What if my wrap rates are too high?

If your company has a high wrap rate, it means you have relatively greater indirect costs and profit that you apply to create fully loaded labor rates. This can be a disadvantage because your competitors can submit lower bids by using lower wrap rates. You can be "underbid" and lose the government contract.

What if my wrap rates are too low?

If your company has a low wrap rate, it means you have relatively less indirect costs and profit. Maybe you can "underbid" your competitors, but maybe your profit margins are smaller.

What is the ideal wrap rate?

There is no such thing as an ideal wrap rate that applies to any company in any industry performing on any contract. The ideal wrap rate is affected by too many factors including the work performed, your competitors, market conditions, and your company's financial position. The only honest answer is "it depends on many factors."

Fine-tuning your wrap rates is an extremely important part of winning government contracts. You need to find a balance between profitability and competitive pricing—the "sweet spot" of wrap rates.

CHAPTER 20, STATING YOUR CASE PERSUASIVELY

How should contractors structure their requests, arguments, claims, or demands?

Organization, structure, clarity, and presentation make all the difference. How you present your argument is just as important as the substance of your argument. If nobody can understand your points, your argument will not convince anyone.

Two identical arguments can be compelling or useless depending on how they are structured. One powerful structure of argument is the syllogism.

What is the syllogism?

Allow me to introduce my friend Aristotle, a Greek genius and polymath who was born in 384 BC. Aristotle was a pupil of Plato, another titan of Greek philosophy. In addition to herculean contributions to philosophy, psychology, mathematics, physics, astronomy, zoology, biology, and political science, Aristotle founded the Western world system of logic and argumentation.

Aristotelian logic provides the syntax and form used to analyze research papers, to distill political campaign arguments, judge legal briefs, compile computer programming language, and to conduct online searches.

What is the major premise, minor premise, and conclusion?

The simplest form of Aristotelian argumentation is the syllogism: major premise, minor premise, and conclusion. For example, all mammals are vertebrates (major premise). A wolf is a mammal (minor premise). Therefore, a wolf must be a vertebrate (conclusion). Note that the conclusion follows necessarily from the major and minor premise; it requires no further argumentation to arrive at the final step.

How can you use syllogisms for government contracting?

The Aristotelian syllogism can be custom tailored for government contracting. The major premise is the rule, and the minor premise is the factual scenario. The conclusion is the major point for you to convey — your "takeaway." The major premise will likely be a citation to a law or regulation. The minor premise may list the relevant circumstances involving the contractor, source selection process, or proposed modification format. As always, the conclusion follows necessarily from the major and minor premises.

Can you provide an example of a government contracting syllogism?

Suppose the government is eager to award your company a $1 million contract. Your company is being pressured to disclose certified cost or pricing data. You think your company need not disclose the certified cost or pricing data. Major premise or rule: The Federal Acquisition Regulation (FAR) states that certified cost or pricing data is required at a threshold of $2 million, provided no exceptions apply. Minor premise or facts: The contract is for $1 million and no exceptions apply. Conclusion: Therefore, certified cost or pricing data is not required.

Why is syllogistic argumentation effective?

Syllogistic argumentation is clear, concise, and commanding. The conclusion is supported by relevant legal or regulatory authority and follows from an orderly chain of thought. Perhaps most important of all, it allows for efficient criticism. If a speaker rambles, backpedals, and trails off into irrelevant tangents, confusion overcomes the audience as it struggles to pinpoint errors or misconceptions.

Using Aristotelian syllogisms, each premise and conclusion is displayed openly to identify problems or misunderstandings immediately.

Why is effective and precise communication so important?

Delivering your arguments with poise, conciseness, and logic will earn you the reputation of a trusted advisor whose analysis is to be treasured. Think before you speak and organize your thoughts before you share them with your colleagues. Using Aristotelian syllogisms and argumentation will allow your research and analytical acuity to stand out, and your public speaking prowess will mark you with distinction.

CHAPTER 21, PRIME CONTRACTORS VERSUS SUBCONTRACTORS

What are the basic differences between performing as a prime contractor versus a subcontractor?

Prime contractors get better profit margins and closer relationships with the government client. Prime contractors also bear the full responsibility for the contract, even if subcontractors fail. Subcontractors give up workshare and profit margins, but they get to work on smaller contracts and avoid having a direct contract with the government, a condition that has significant advantages. Many government contracting companies start with subcontracts to gain experience and confidence, and then pursue prime contracts later.

How many contractors does it take to perform a government contract?

This question evokes the corny joke about "How many contractors does it take to screw in a light bulb?" But seriously, you need to understand the layers of prime contracts, subcontracts, and lower-tier subcontracts.

Government contracts are often performed by several different companies in a cascading pattern. The first contractor wins a government contract. The first contractor is known as the prime contractor.

The prime contractor cannot or does not want to perform 100 percent of the work, so the prime contractor finds a second contractor to perform a portion of the work. The second contractor is known as the subcontractor.

When the first contractor (prime contractor) and second contractor (subcontractor) sign a contract to perform some of the work — a portion of the original government prime contract — that is called a *subcontract*.

Is "subcontract" a relative term?

Yes, the term *subcontract* is always relative to the original contract with the government. The subcontractor, of course, can also subcontract a portion of its work to other companies. "Subcontract of a subcontract" sounds awkward, so you call it a *2nd-tier subcontract* performed by a *2nd-tier subcontractor*.

The 2nd-tier subcontractor, of course, can also subcontract a portion of its work to a 3rd-tier subcontractor, and so forth. The various "tiers" or "levels" of subcontracting indicate the distance from the original government contract, which is a contract between the government and the prime contractor.

What can the children's "telephone game" illustrate to you about government contracting?

As you now understand, *subcontract* is a relative term. Subcontractor to whom? The farther away your company is from the prime contract with the government, the more complicated the business relationship. Just like the "telephone game" that children play, the original message from the government is likely to change as it passes from prime contractor to subcontractor to 2nd-tier subcontractor. Beware this phenomenon.

Always be skeptical when your prime contractor describes messages that allegedly came from the government. There is a very good chance that the original message from the government was distorted or changed by one of the middlemen. Any distortion is likeliest to benefit the prime contractor, and not your subcontracting company. Be skeptical!

What is privity of contract?

Only the prime contractor has a direct contractual relationship with the government client. This direct contractual relationship is called *privity of contract* — an important concept to understand. If you have a contract with another party, then you have *privity of contract* with that other party. The two of you share a relationship in that you are both parties to a single contract that applies to both of you.

Does a subcontractor have privity of contract with the government?

No! The prime contractor has *privity of contract* with the government. The prime contractor also has *privity of contract* with the subcontractor. However, the subcontractor does not have privity of contract with the government. The subcontractor only has a direct contractual relationship with the prime contractor, in the form of a subcontract. You must understand this dynamic.

Although a subcontractor may also support the government client, there is only one prime contractor. The risk of failure for the entire government contract belongs to the prime contractor, not the subcontractor. As a prime contractor, blaming a subcontractor, even if the subcontractor fails, is simply not an option. The prime contractor bears all the risk and responsibility for its entire chain of subcontracts.

What are the advantages of being the prime contractor?

With greater risk comes greater rewards. Prime contractors have several advantages over subcontractors. Your cash flow is better because you get paid first. Imagine being a 3rd-tier subcontractor. The 3rd-tier subcontractor waits for the prime contractor to get paid, then the subcontractor, then the 2nd-tier subcontractor. You're lucky if each stage takes only 30 days. These delays are why the negotiation of payment terms is so important to your company cash flow.

Not only is the prime contractor paid first, it also gets the lion's share of the profits. Any subcontractor is negotiating for a subset or fraction of the entire profit of the government contract — whatever the prime contractor is willing to subcontract away. Profit margins for lower tier subcontractors usually get smaller and smaller as each middleman takes a cut.

Prime contractors are closer to the government client. The United States of America is the largest client in world history. It pays to work with a client that spends more than a trillion dollars every year through government contracts and grants. Your book of business can grow as contact with one federal agency leads to new work or new clients at other federal agencies.

CHAPTER 22, GOVERNMENT PERSPECTIVE

What is the government's relative negotiation strength?

Very strong! When you are the only seller, you have a *monopoly*. When you are the only buyer, you have a *monopsony*. The US federal government is the largest client in the history of the world, spending more than one trillion dollars per year. You may have heard the expression, "It's good to be the King." The federal government holds a significant advantage because it writes rules that favor itself, spends taxpayer money, and can move on to the next contractor. While there are tens of thousands of government contractors, there is only one federal government.

What is the government's negotiation strength with sole-source companies?

The government advantage is reversed if your company is the only source for a product or service. As the sole source, contractors can flex their negotiation muscles and demand exceptional terms or prices. When evaluating your negotiation position, think about who can walk away from the deal. Even if you are not the only source, your bargaining power increases with fewer competitors.

Does the government have significant flexibility in negotiating contracts?

No, not when compared to private-sector contracts. Federal government procurement contracts have cookie-cutter clauses that permit little creativity or critical thinking.

These standardized clauses are found in the Federal Acquisition Regulation (FAR). The contracting officer follows the direction of the FAR, which explains when to use which clause, depending on the nature and attributes of the contract.

Although many FAR clauses are predefined, contracting officers have considerable flexibility to negotiate the period of performance, payment structure, and the Statement of Work. However, a FAR-based government contract is strictly limited in what can be included, omitted, or changed regarding individual FAR clauses.

For these reasons, contractors should focus on what they can influence. Contractors can negotiate pricing terms, delivery schedules, performance standards, and other elements of the contract. Also consider that you can influence contract terms based on what you include in the contractor proposal to the government.

When is the contractor's window of opportunity to negotiate prime contract terms?

By the time the contractor receives a government contract to sign, most opportunities to negotiate have disappeared. Your time to negotiate is when you submit the proposal and when you negotiate price or proposal changes. Therefore, most contractor-to-government negotiation is complete by the time the contract is offered for signature.

Do sole-source contracts offer more opportunities to negotiate?

Yes, if only your company can perform the contract, your company has an extraordinary amount of negotiation leverage. In sole-source contracts, the government is forced to negotiate because there is no alternative.

What is the J&A or Justification and Approval for Other Than Full and Open Competition?

You may have heard of the *Justification and Approval for Other Than Full and Open Competition,* also called the *J&A.* The J&A explains why the government has little or no competitive alternatives to your company, which justifies noncompetitive procurements such as *sole-source contracts.* If you are the sole source listed in a *J&A* or similar document, adjust your negotiation strategy accordingly. Ask for more than you would in competitive procurements because there are no alternatives. Sole-source contracts can demand better pricing, schedules, and terms than other contracts — but only if you request these changes through negotiation.

If the government has barely any flexibility, how should contractors request changes to FAR clauses?

First, remember that executing any changes to the contract are infinitely easier before you sign. After you sign the contract, it will be an uphill battle to make any changes because you have no negotiation power. The government contracting officer can always respond to your request for changes by saying, "You should have identified this problem before you signed the contract. Now you have agreed to the deal as written."

Second, prioritize changing only the most important clauses. If you expect to have any FAR clauses deleted or changed, choose your battles. Expect to find in the contract several FAR clauses that are incorrect or inappropriate under the circumstances of your contract.

You may need to ignore several glaring errors to focus instead on the few clauses that will cause you the most severe problems. Focus on errors in price, delivery, inspection, acceptance, the statement of work or specifications, and the ability to terminate the contract. Remember that overworked contracting officers are more likely to accept changes that are quick and easy to fix. Focus on the "big-ticket items" and ignore minor mistakes.

What are the government's contracting priorities?

Speed, volume, and compliance. Be skeptical about what the Federal Acquisition Regulation (FAR) states about government contracting priorities because those words are lofty slogans, not reality. The naïve will believe the text of FAR Part 1 (Federal Acquisition Regulations System), which includes the "Statement of guiding principles." These principles include promoting competition, minimizing operating costs, conducting business with integrity, and fulfilling policy objectives. While most government employees strive to achieve these lofty goals, try to be more realistic. Rather than aspirational public policy, think about the practical priorities of managers who want to please their superiors.

The government cares about speed, volume, and compliance. Notice that compliance is directly opposed to speed because working faster may involve shortcuts or carelessness. Therefore, the government must balance competing priorities.

Compliance is mostly enforced by the stick, rather than carrot. In other words, contracting officers do not want to be caught making mistakes and contracting leaders do not want to be embarrassed by their staff.

No rewards exist for following the rules, but there are serious penalties for breaking the rules. As a result, many contracting officers are risk-averse and cautious.

Speed and volume are important to the contracting team's larger customer, which is the program office or the entire agency. Contracting departments issue contracts to support the mission of the federal agency or particular goals of individual programs or projects. As such, the contracting department is considered *support staff*. For example, the Federal Bureau of Investigation (FBI) prioritizes its field agents because they execute the mission of the FBI — investigating federal crimes. The contracting department simply purchases whatever is necessary to accomplish the mission, and the FBI wants these contracts completed quickly.

How does the government measure productivity and output for contracting?

The faster the contract is negotiated and signed, the faster the contracting officer can move to the next contract. The simplest metric for success is the number of new contracts signed, or the number of individual *contract actions* (including modifications). Typically, the government measures productivity by counting new contracts signed and contract actions (like modifications) during a fiscal year.

What is the fiscal year for the US federal government?

The US government fiscal year is October 1 through September 30. Fiscal year 2099 will start on October 1, 2098, and end on September 30, 2099.

How can a contractor help the government with its priority of speed and volume?

Never delay the process. Always have your research, conclusions, and requests prepared before any meeting or interaction. Meet your deadlines. Do not waste the contracting officer's time. The contracting department is extremely busy. You will not be respected if you cause delays or create extra work. Do your best to make the negotiation and administration of contracts as easy as possible while still protecting your business interests.

How can a contractor help the government with its priority of compliance?

The government's third priority is compliance. Faced with countless laws, regulations, policies, and court decisions, the contracting officer wants to avoid breaking rules or inviting further scrutiny from outside auditors.

Sometimes the government contracting officer may feel uncomfortable performing an action or using a process that is new or unfamiliar, although it is perfectly legitimate and complies with the rules. You can help by providing that contracting officer with the research and conclusions that justify the particular action. In other words, make their lives easier by doing their jobs for them. Share your careful research and references with the contracting officer. Painstakingly outline your requests and their justifications. Summarize your findings with a clear subject line and helpful headers between sections. Anticipate the government's compliance workload and try to perform as many helpful steps as possible.

How should contractors communicate with the government client?

Your written communication with the government must be persuasive, precise, prudent, and professional. Always include references and suitable citations. State your case in logical sequence. Value government client time as much as your own.

Effective communication is vital to your success with the government client. Much can be lost to ineffective translation. Do not let that happen. Review the chapter, "Stating Your Case Persuasively."

Should contractors take special precaution to use the correct words, terms, and definitions?

Yes, use words carefully. Respect and adhere to specific definitions for words and terms of art in the government contracting industry. Terms like *claim*, *subcontract*, and *quote* have very specific meanings. These meanings can change depending on new circumstances and application. Always recognize the context in which you use words and terms.

Why should contractors "measure twice, cut once" with emails and letters?

Do not overwhelm the government client with emails or letters. This rookie mistake will doom your company to being ignored and avoided. Many government contractors seek my consulting services because the government client ignored them for weeks or months. This kind of dismissal is often because the government client is over worked and overscheduled. Another possibility is the government client is tired of too many email messages from the contractor. In either case, problems can be avoided.

"Measure twice, cut once" is advice for construction and carpentry. The idea is to plan your next move carefully, so that you do not make a mistake. This maxim applies to written communications with the government client. Think carefully and review each email message or letter painstakingly before you send it to the government client.

Your goal is to become respected as an excellent writer and communicator. This goal means writing three sentences rather than a full page. This goal means completing phone calls in 10 minutes rather than 1 hour. Finally, this goal means a reputation for flawless communications in writing. Your government client is busy, and you want to make life for the client easier, not harder. If you are not a strong writer or communicator, hire a competent professional to help you.

How should contractors say "No" during negotiation with the government?

Nobody wants to say "No" to the government client. Better to offer a solution different from what was proposed, rather than flat-out saying "No."

Propose a better idea while carefully pointing out the risks or weaknesses of the idea you turn down. Nobody wants a person who always says "No." Conversely, the person who always has sensible solutions and creative ideas is always in demand.

How can you learn to speak and understand the language of government contracting?

Your government client, especially the contracting officer, speaks a language different from yours. This foreign language is called *government contracts*. People who speak English can barely communicate with those who speak the language of government contracts, and complex conversations are nearly impossible.

Reading this book is a great start, but you should also read my bestselling first two books, *Government Contracts in Plain English* (available at https://www.amazon.com/dp/173419815X/) and *Federal Acquisition Regulation in Plain English* (available at https://www.amazon.com/dp/1734198117). Buy every book in *The Government Contracts in Plain English Series*: https://www.amazon.com/dp/B09MRCMWBD

Learn to speak and understand the language of government contracts or find yourself a competent professional translator. You must understand key terms of art and critical concepts. Otherwise, you will miss subtle indicators and your inexperience may frustrate your government client.

CHAPTER 23, PRIME CONTRACTOR PERSPECTIVE

What are the priorities of the prime contractor when negotiating with the government?

Preserve the relationship! You will negotiate with scores of other contractors but there is only one Uncle Sam. The US federal government is the largest client in the history of mankind, spending more than $1 trillion every year. Your company wants to be a recurring vendor that wins multiple contracts over many years. For these reasons, value the long-term relationship more than you value any individual contract or transaction. Fancy academics call this *relational* rather than *transactional* contracting.

What are the priorities of the prime contractor when negotiating with a subcontractor?

Prime contractors need subcontractors who will reliably perform the work. The first priority is to thoroughly vet any subcontractor's capabilities and past performance to ensure they can perform successfully. Remember the prime contractor is responsible for the success or failure of all its subcontractors in a government contract. Blaming the subcontractor is never a valid excuse; rather, the prime contractor assumes the risk of subcontractors. For these reasons, choose your subcontractors carefully.

Beyond competency, prime contractors need to shift risk to subcontractors and *flow down* any required Federal Acquisition Regulation (FAR) clauses.

What does it mean for a prime contractor to "flow down" a FAR clause into a subcontract?

Generally, a *flow-down clause* is any contract clause that a prime contractor or subcontractor duplicates in a subcontract with a lower tier subcontractor. For example, let's say clause XYZ is in the prime contractor's government contract with US Department of Justice. If the prime contractor *flows down* clause XYZ by including it in a subcontract, clause XYZ is a flow-down clause. The prime contractor "flows down" clause XYZ from its government contract to its subcontractor. Both the government contract (between Department of Justice and prime contractor) and the subcontract (between prime contractor and subcontractor) have some version of clause XYZ. Therefore, clause XYZ has *flowed down* to the subcontractor. Learn more by reading the chapter, "Flow-Down Clauses."

Should prime contractors flow down some form of the Termination clause?

Yes, the most important FAR clause to flow down to subcontractors is some form of the Termination for Convenience clause. If this termination clause is in your prime contract, you need to include it in related subcontracts. Read more about termination clauses—and why you need them in subcontracts—in the chapter, "Noteworthy FAR Clauses."

Should prime contractors flow down to subcontractors every FAR clause from the prime contract?

No, prime contractors must carefully choose and tailor every flow-down clause.

How does the prime contractor know whether a FAR clause must be flowed down to subcontractors?

Learn more about *flow-down prescription clauses* in the chapter, "Flow-Down Clauses." These *flow-down prescription clauses* are found within the text of some FAR clauses. If that FAR clause is in your prime contract, the text within it may direct you to *flow down* some version of the clause into subcontracts.

Are you saying prime contractors need to carefully evaluate every single FAR clause they flow down to subcontractors?

Yes, prime contractors need to evaluate each FAR clause to determine whether it should or must be flowed down to subcontracts. This process requires painstaking, precise work.

Should prime contractors flow down the entire FAR, just to play it safe?

No, absolutely not! Some prime contractors include a blanket statement like "the entire Federal Acquisition Regulation (FAR) is incorporated into this subcontract" or "all FAR clauses apply to this subcontract." Never use this language. Never try to incorporate the entire FAR into any contract or subcontract. If you do so, you announce your incompetency and your fundamental ignorance of government contracting.

Why is this idea foolish and nonsensical?

Not only is the idea of incorporating the entire FAR foolish, the concept is also incoherent. The idea is foolish because it creates additional risk and terribly confuses the terms of the contract. The FAR contains hundreds of conflicting and mutually exclusive FAR clauses, so the concept is nonsensical. Use your judgment and avoid signing any contract or subcontract that includes "the entire FAR."

What is the relative negotiation strength of the prime contractor?

Prime contractors have significant leverage over subcontractors. The prime contractor holds the complete government contract, while the subcontractors fight for scraps from the table, hoping for a portion thereof. While subcontractors can be replaced, the prime contractor is the single point of contact for the government client. For these reasons, prime contractors have the advantage over subcontractors during most negotiations. Prime contractors can dictate terms, threaten to withdraw, present their model contract format first, and exercise many other privileges. Perhaps the most powerful advantage is that the prime contractor controls the entire scope of work, and can choose to delegate as much or as little — or nothing — to subcontractors.

Is the prime contractor usually a larger company than the subcontractor?

Often the prime contractor is a larger or more experienced company than the subcontractor, but this rule is not universal. Many subcontractors are larger than the prime contractor. In fact, one common arrangement is that a small business prime contractor engages a larger company as the subcontractor. The small business is eligible for special *small business set-aside contracts* where larger companies cannot compete. In those situations, the large company is happy to serve as the subcontractor because it is the only option to perform the underlying work. If your small business wins these set-asides, you are the only channel for large businesses to participate. Read more about these small business benefits and teaming arrangements in *Government Contracts in Plain English*, available at https://www.amazon.com/dp/173419815X/.

CHAPTER 24, SUBCONTRACTOR PERSPECTIVE

What is the relative negotiation strength of the subcontractor?

Weak! Usually, the subcontractor has less negotiation leverage when compared to the prime contractor. The prime contractor holds the entire contract with the government client and exercises wide discretion in choosing subcontractors and tailoring clauses for the subcontract. If the potential subcontractor demands too much during subcontract negotiation, the prime contractor can dump them and look elsewhere. For these reasons, subcontractors must tread carefully during subcontract negotiation.

How should subcontractors approach subcontract negotiation?

Choose your battles. Expect that you will not be granted all your wishes, so prioritize the most important changes. Evaluate the likelihood of risk and monetary cost of every change you request. Focus on the big-ticket items that can jeopardize performance, payment, or cause your company serious problems.

When will the subcontractor hold negotiation leverage over the prime?

The exception to the rule that prime contractors have stronger negotiating power is when the subcontractor is one of the only possible sources to perform the work. In those exceptional cases, the subcontractor may be able to dictate terms to the prime contractor.

Perhaps the most advantageous position of a subcontractor is when the government client of the prime contractor has explicitly or implicitly requested the performance of a specific subcontractor. If you are the favored source for the government client, the prime contractor has every incentive to secure your services by negotiating a favorable subcontract.

What sections should the subcontractor prioritize?

Subcontractors need to pay close attention to payment terms. Your payment can be significantly delayed if other parties must be paid before your company gets paid. Avoid these "pay when paid" contract terms like the plague! Instead, negotiate payment based on definite timelines that leave no contingencies to other parties. Learn more about these concepts by reviewing the chapter, "Getting Paid: Invoice and Payment Terms."

Should subcontractors be careful about accepting flow-down clauses?

Yes, subcontractors need to be vigilant about any Federal Acquisition Regulation (FAR) clauses the prime contractor wants to *flow down* into the subcontract. Some FAR clauses must be included in subcontracts, some are optional, and some never belong in any subcontracts. To understand which situation applies, read the chapters, "Flow-Down Clauses" and "The Myth of Self-Deleting Clauses."

Should subcontractors review every single flow-down clause?

Yes! Subcontractors should review each flow-down clause to verify it belongs in the subcontract. If the flow-down clause does not belong or is not appropriately tailored, you should delete or change the clause.

Ask the prime contractor to justify why any clause should or must be flowed down to the subcontractor. Do not accept answers like, "Our company sent you the standard subcontract" or "Our company flows down all those clauses in every subcontract." You need specific justifications outlined in the chapters, "Prescription Clauses" and "Flow-Down Clauses."

What are the advantages of being a subcontractor?

Maybe you don't want to do business with the government. Remember, a subcontractor does not have "privity of contract" or a direct contractual relationship with the government. That lack of a direct contractual relationship can be a significant advantage.

As a subcontractor, you have a contract simply with another private business. If you have problems or litigation, you are subject to private sector contract law rather than federal contract law. As a professor and expert witness in federal contract law, I can assure you that several aspects of federal contract law favor the government and not the contractors.

Subcontractors can avoid most of the aspects of federal contract law that heavily favor the government. A subcontract between two businesses will be subject to the same legal conventions as any other private sector contract. Litigation between two subcontractors (or between a prime contractor and subcontractor) will often take place in state court, rather than federal court. In contrast, contract litigation between a prime contractor and the federal government will be subject to federal contract law, and will likely take place in federal court.

Subcontractors have greater freedom to design contract terms. Government contracts with the prime contractor are bound by strict regulations like the Federal Acquisition Regulation (FAR), but subcontracts have more flexibility. Take advantage of this flexibility whenever possible. Negotiate terms that protect you as a subcontractor. For more information, read the chapter, "Flow-Down Clauses."

Your negotiating position will likely be weak in relation to the prime contractor or a higher tier subcontractor. Do not let the prime contractor push you into an unfavorable subcontract. Be prepared to walk away, if necessary. Another advantage of being a subcontractor is the reserved power to choose your contracts carefully, and to walk away from unwise opportunities or shady business partners.

Subcontractors can get a foot in the door by performing smaller portions of government contracts without shouldering all the risk and responsibility. Subcontractors can target new types of work and gain valuable experience and contacts while avoiding the crushing possibility of failure in front of the government client. In this way, subcontractors can practice in the minor leagues (subcontracts with other companies) before stepping up to the major leagues (prime contracts with the government).

Is the subcontractor contractually responsible for the prime contractor's performance?

No. The subcontractor is contractually responsible only for the (sub)contract between the prime contractor and subcontractor. The (sub)contract is usually a portion or fraction of the entire prime contract between the government and the prime contractor. The prime contractor cannot or will not perform the entire prime contract, so the prime contractor *subcontracts* some of the work to another company (the subcontractor).

The subcontract is a "slice of the pie," not the entire pie (the entire prime contract with the government). However, the prime contractor hires the subcontractor as one part of a larger effort to perform the prime contract. The subcontractor's success in performing the "slice of the pie" is integral to the prime contractor's success in performing the entire prime contract.

Will the prime contractor be upset if the subcontractor's failure to perform affects the prime contract negatively?

Yes, but the word "upset" is not the right word. The prime contractor will be *livid* (enraged, furious, very angry!) if the subcontractor's failure hurts the prime contractor's performance.

Why will the prime contractor be so angry at the subcontractor for failure to perform the subcontract?

When performing the prime contract with the government, the prime contractor is responsible for all subcontractors' performances. The failure of any subcontractor is the prime contractor's problem. The government will blame the prime contractor, not the subcontractor.

The prime contractor cannot shift blame successfully to subcontractors. In fact, the very first words of a FAR clause called "Excusable Delays" begin with "Except for defaults of subcontractors at any tier..." and continues to list justifiable (excusable) reasons for prime contractor failure. Therefore, the government has the explicit policy for prime contractors: *Don't try to blame your subcontractors!*

Chapter 25, Contractor Employee Perspective

What is a contractor employee in this context of government contract negotiation?

A contractor employee works for a company that has a prime contract (or subcontract) with the government. This person is an employee of a company that acts as a contractor (or subcontractor). This person does not own this company, and this company did not sign a subcontract with the employee. A traditional employer-employee relationship exists, with a salary and benefits. The company pays the salary, withholds tax, and may contribute to the employee's retirement plan.

What are the shorthand terms to distinguish employees from independent contractors?

Some describe the traditional employment relationship as *W-2* because of the Internal Revenue Service W-2 tax form for employees. In contrast, independent contractors use *1099* tax forms because they are not employees. If you want to negotiate as an independent contractor, you should also read the chapter, "Sole Proprietor Perspective."

What is the relative negotiation strength of the contractor employee?

Weak! Individual contractor employees are replaceable. However, the exception to this rule applies when your job is highly specialized. If you have niche, in-demand skills and experience, your negotiation position will improve.

When should contractor employees negotiate?

Negotiate before you start your job! Pay, working conditions, location, benefits, job duties, reporting responsibilities, and other such matters should be negotiated before you accept employment. After you start the job, it will be harder to negotiate salary increases or other changes. Negotiate from the start of the process!

Should you take the first offer of employment?

If you think you can get a better offer without losing the opportunity, make a counteroffer. Many employees are afraid to negotiate their salary or benefits. Some fear the company will retract the job offer. Companies that value employee retention and satisfaction will not be offended by counteroffers or requests for salary increases. If you make a counteroffer, be respectful and emphasize your interest and fitness for the position.

Is your primary loyalty to the company or to the government client?

If your job is onsite or working directly with the government client, your primary loyalty may reside with the government client instead of your current employer. Although your employer signs your checks and pays your benefits, you understand that the primary source of your funding comes from the government client.

In some cases, even if your employer loses the contract, you will find a new job with the next company that does win the contract. Contractor employees frequently switch employers simply to stay with the same government client. Sometimes the individual contractor employees enjoy longer tenure and stronger client loyalty than the contractor company. While the company must recompete to win the contract every 5 years, the employee can switch employers repeatedly yet continue working with the same government client for decades.

What is the relative negotiation strength of an incumbent contractor employee?

Stronger! When a new company wins a government contract previously performed by a competitor, the new company often wants to secure the *incumbent* contractor employees. If you are the incumbent — currently performing on a government contract — the successor contractor wants you to join their successor company. If you were successful in the prior contract working for the prior contractor, the next contractor will want you on its team.

When negotiating your employment terms with the successor contractor, remember that your negotiation position is stronger. You have demonstrated success. The government client knows you and likes you. You hold extremely valuable information about the government client and its specific needs, preferences, and operations.

Does the dual loyalty of their employees pose a challenge to onsite government contractors?

Yes, government contractors that provide onsite support to government clients wrestle with the issue of their employees becoming more loyal to the government client.

Some companies directly address this problem by involving employees in companywide events, requiring regular meetings at the corporate office, or other activities designed to connect the employee to the company culture. Other companies think that their employees who work onsite with the government are replaceable, not loyal, and therefore not worth the effort. I recommend that companies make every effort to include all employees in corporate activities—especially onsite contractors. Otherwise, the company will lose many employees to competitor companies or to employment with the government client. Maintaining your workforce is cheaper and easier than continually replacing it.

Does the government often hire contractor employees for federal civilian employee positions?

Yes, the government often hires the employees of contractors for government jobs in the federal civilian service. This possibility is one more reason why contractor employees may value the government client more than their current employer.

Why would a contractor employee quit to become a government employee?

Although contractor employees sometimes make more money than their government employee equivalents, government employment is significantly more stable and usually provides superior benefits. Contractor employees are usually *at will*, meaning the company can fire you at any time for almost any reason. In contrast, it is difficult to fire a government employee. The benefits for government employees are extraordinary, including paid overtime for salaried positions, discounted health insurance, and generous vacation and sick leave.

What should a contractor employee consider when negotiating for a job with a government contractor company?

Obviously the most important topic for negotiation is your salary. But do not ignore other aspects such as paid leave (sick leave and vacation), medical benefits, retirement plan contributions, parking or commuting reimbursements, and telework flexibility.

What should contractor employees understand about medical benefits and health insurance?

If you or your spouse have access to medical benefits or health insurance from an alternative source, you cost the company less to employ you. If the company need not pay for your health insurance, you can ask for a corresponding offset in another area, such as your salary. Ask for a slightly higher salary to forgo other benefits.

Will you help me negotiate my next job, revise my resume, improve my interview skills, or achieve my career goals? I do not own a company. I just need help!

Sure, maybe. I have helped many individual people — both government employees and industry contractors — achieve their professional goals, including resume revisions, interview coaching, and long-term career planning. Send me an email: Christoph@ChristophLLC.com.

Chapter 26, Sole Proprietor Perspective

What is a sole proprietor in this context of government contract negotiation?

In this context of this chapter, *sole proprietor* means an individual who is self-employed or a company of which the sole owner is also the only employee. The prime contractor (or another subcontractor) subcontracts with an individual person or with a company that is 100 percent owned by one person who is the sole employee of that company.

Distinguish the sole proprietor from the subcontractor described in the chapter, "Subcontractor Perspective." The difference is that the subcontractor has multiple employees rather than operating as a one-man show. Also distinguish the sole proprietor from the chapter, "Contractor Employee Perspective." The difference is the contractor employee enters an employer-employee relationship, while a sole proprietor signs a contract (as an *independent contractor*).

Can you provide some examples of sole proprietorship in this context?

Boeing wins a $200 million prime contract with the Department of Defense. Boeing will subcontract a portion of the work to you as a sole proprietor. You have highly specialized skills in cybersecurity, so you are the only qualified person for this subcontracted portion of the work. In this matter, you have two choices.

(1) You can sign the subcontract personally, using your full name and assuming personal responsibility. By signing personally, you are an individual acting as a sole proprietor. Boeing enters into a subcontract with you as an individual who is self-employed.

(2) Your other choice is to form a limited liability company (LLC) that is owned 100 percent by you that has only one employee (you). Using the LLC, you can sign the subcontract on behalf of the LLC, rather than personally. Boeing enters into a subcontract with your company, not with you. Despite your complete ownership of the company that employs only you, the company is responsible for any problems or litigation arising under the subcontract. For this reason, many sole proprietors choose to create a company rather than operating as an individual. For more information about the legal, tax, and liability benefits of forming a company, you need to consult a business attorney or certified public accountant (CPA).

Please note that in this context, *sole proprietor* is distinguished from multiple-employee companies and from employees of other contracting companies. The term *sole proprietor* has other tax, legal, and business definitions that this book cannot explore.

What is the relative negotiation strength of the sole proprietor?

Weak. The negotiation strength of the sole proprietor is somewhere between a subcontractor and contractor employee. The sole proprietor is a single person but must negotiate favorable terms with a prime contractor with many more employees and resources.

Do sole proprietors "survive contract-by-contract?"

Yes, in many cases, sole proprietors "survive contract-by-contract." Sole proprietors must continually find and win contracts. While employees work for a company that performs business development, this responsibility rests completely with the sole proprietor. The loss of one large (sub)contract can be devastating to a sole proprietor if that single (sub)contract represents the lion's share of revenue.

Are sole proprietors more flexible in their contracting relationships?

Yes, sole proprietors have considerable freedom to change their contracting relationships. While employees are subject to the policies of their employers, sole proprietors set their own policies. Sole proprietors can more easily start, stop, or change existing contracting relationships. Finally, sole proprietors have no bureaucracy to slow down decisions. The sole proprietor makes all decisions.

What if my company employs other people, not only me?

If your company has any other employee(s), you should read the chapter, "Subcontractor Perspective." This chapter focuses on individuals and companies owned by one person that employ only that same person.

What are the pros and cons of being a sole proprietor versus an employee?

As an employee of a government contractor or subcontractor, you work for that company, not for yourself. The company pays your salary, provides you paid vacation and sick leave, and offers health care and retirement benefits.

Being an employee of a company provides more stability than working for yourself. In addition to regular salary and benefits, the company spends time and resources to secure future business, revenue, and profits. As the employee, you focus on your job while the company worries about marketing, winning future contracts, and operating a profitable business.

As a sole proprietor, you are responsible for achieving everything discussed previously. Your salary, vacation, health care, retirement, marketing, revenue, and profitability are all in your hands. Business ownership is a serious commitment of time.

Is a sole proprietor self-employed?

Yes. As a sole proprietor, you work for yourself. You are self-employed, so nobody pays your salary, provides vacation and sick leave, or offers health care and retirement benefits. Instead, all these responsibilities are yours. You must decide how to apportion these costs from your total earnings.

While an employee enters into an employment relationship, the sole proprietor typically enters into a contract. The employee signs up for a job with a company. The sole proprietor enters into a contractual relationship with a company. Recruiters distinguish these two working relationships as *W-2* (employer-employee) or *1099* (independent contractor).

How should sole proprietors structure their rates and fees?

The sole proprietor must consider the costs of non-salary benefits like health insurance, vacation, and other costs of running a business.

The self-employed person should structure their compensation to cover the costs of running a business and providing non-salary benefits. For example, an employee who earns $200,000 per year also receives tens of thousands of dollars in non-salary benefits, such as health insurance, paid vacation, and pension matching. This employee's total salary and benefits is therefore greater than $200,000 per year.

The self-employed sole proprietor must provide any benefits out of pocket, so the compensation for the same position should be greater than $200,000 per year. To think through these calculations, read the chapter, "Negotiating Labor Rates and Wrap Rates."

Should I become a sole proprietor and quit my employment?

Maybe. There is no universal answer to this question.

Will you help me explore the possibility of self-employment and sole proprietorship?

Sure, maybe. Send me an email: Christoph@ChristophLLC.com. I have helped many individuals achieve their professional goals, like starting their own business, setting up a business banking account, finding a good accountant, and negotiating a contract rather than employment. I know the process of shifting to self-employment and starting a small business because I did all that with www.ChristophLLC.com.

Why do prime contractors distinguish sole proprietors from smaller companies that have multiple employees?

Prime contractors distinguish sole proprietors (whether individual consultants or companies owned by a single person with one employee) from multiple-employee companies for several reasons. First, a sole proprietor poses less of a threat to the prime contractor. As a sole proprietor, you offer a single full-time equivalent (FTE) labor unit — merely one job or employment position. If you owned a company that employs several other people, your company represents multiple jobs or employment positions. Therefore, your company may *poach* or steal employees from the prime contractor or poach future government contracts that the prime contractor would have secured. In contrast, sole proprietors are less of a threat to prime contractors.

Second, a sole proprietor can be classified by the prime contractor as a consultant rather than a subcontractor. Do not confuse this internal classification by the prime contractor with the (sub)contractual relationship. Although you or your company will sign a subcontract, some prime contractors view one-person enterprises as "consultants" in their internal documentation. This classification as a consultant can be related to several factors, including taxation, cost allocation, complexity of the subcontract, and how the prime contractor charges the government client for the costs of your subcontract.

CHAPTER 27, COMMON CONTRACT SECTIONS IN PLAIN ENGLISH

This chapter delivers a plain English explanation for the most common contract sections or clauses. By learning the meaning and context for these frequently used clauses, you will gain confidence and new insights for future negotiations. At the very least, you will understand the contracts better that you negotiate, sign, and perform! If you need help with your government contracting issues, hire a professional. Send your email to Christoph@ChristophLLC.com.

Acceptance. Remember that acceptance clauses may control if and when you will be paid! If your products or services are not accepted — which means they are rejected — the client may have the right to withhold payment. Do not accept vague or ambiguous acceptance sections. Make sure it is abundantly clear what action or inaction constitutes acceptance. For example, if you deliver and hear nothing for one week, does that mean the delivery is accepted? Or do you require written proof of affirmative acceptance?

Also consider the timeline to provide or withhold acceptance after delivery and inspection. Negotiate reductions to any excessively long timelines. Again, you do not want the acceptance process to delay your payment. Acceptance should be required a few days after the time period required for inspection, which has its own section in this chapter. You can read more about delivery, inspection, and acceptance in the earlier chapter, "Noteworthy FAR Clauses."

Announcements (see publicity or public notices)

Approval of lower tier subcontractors. Some contracts require approval for the addition of any other subcontractors. For whatever reason, the prime contractor does not want the subcontractor to further subcontract or delegate any of the work without permission. If you sign such a clause, carefully review exactly what you must submit, who has the power to approve, and how long the approval process will take. Negotiating a new subcontract is difficult enough without the added complication of requiring approval by a third party.

The government occasionally requires approval of lower-tier subcontractors for similar reasons. If the work is sensitive or critical to the agency mission, the government eliminates additional risk by carefully vetting any subcontractors. For that reason, the prime contractor must ask for government permission to enroll any subcontractors.

Assignment clauses address the ability to transfer the contract to a third party who has not signed the contract. When you read *assignment*, think about one party to the contract substituting another party for itself. The assignment (transfer) to a new party makes the new party "step into the shoes" of the original signer, inheriting both the rights and obligations to perform.

Usually, assignment clauses limit or prevent the ability to transfer the contract. Many contractors want the contract to remain between the original two parties (rather than a third-party transferee). If you have no assignment clause in your contract, it may be possible to transfer the contract to another person or company. Now you know why many contracts include limitations on assignment!

Remember that contracts consist of rights (what you can do) and obligations (what you must do). Stated differently, your rights are your powers to act and your obligations are your responsibilities to perform. You may want your assignment clause to carefully address both the assignment of rights (what you can do) and the assignment of obligations (what you must do). In legal jargon, often the rights are assigned, but the duties are *delegated*. Therefore, if you state only that "assignments are limited," someone could misinterpret your intent by thinking that only the assignment of rights is limited but the assignment of obligations is not limited. Your contract could be interpreted as allowing the assignment (delegation) of obligations simply because you forgot to use the magic word of *delegation*. The easy solution is to write your assignment clause to include both words: rights and obligations. For example, "The parties shall not assign any of the rights or obligations of this contract." This method prevents any confusion or misinterpretation.

Attorneys' fees sections address who will pay the costs of legal services if the contract spirals into lawsuits. Of course, if there is no special agreement about attorneys' fees, your company pays its own legal fees and the other company pays its own. Paying your own legal fees, rather than the fees of others, is known as the *American rule* to distinguish the situation from practices in some other countries. In other countries, sometimes the loser of a lawsuit must pay the loser's own legal fees and also pay the other side's legal fees.

If you want each party to be responsible for its own attorneys' fees, you can reinforce this *American rule* in the attorneys' fees section. In contrast, you can force the loser of a lawsuit to pay for both parties' legal fees by writing that contingency into the attorneys' fees clause. By making the loser pay for the other side's legal fees, this arrangement increases the cost of litigation and deters unnecessary or meritless lawsuits. If you know you must pay two sets of attorneys' fees if you lose, you are less likely to initiate litigation.

Business-to-business is a category of activity where companies provide goods or services to other companies. For example, www.ChristophLLC.com operates in a business-to-business capacity because my company provides expert advice to other government contracting companies. If your company sells to other companies, it can be described as business-to-business. Business-to-business is abbreviated as "B2B."

Business-to-consumer means the company sells directly to the consumer with no middlemen. Very few companies are actually business-to-consumer. Most manufacturers employ middlemen distributors or retail agents to complete the chain of sale from creator to consumer. Business-to-consumer is abbreviated as "B2C."

Business-to-government means the company sells directly to the government. Government contractors holding a prime contract are, by definition, business-to-government. If your company participates in government contracting strictly as a subcontractor, things become complicated and nuanced.

Although your goods and services may end up with the government client, your contract with another company means you are actually *business-to-business* (B2B). To be truly business-to-government, your company must hold a prime contract rather than perform as a subcontractor. *Business-to-government* is abbreviated as "B2G." Many companies operate as both "B2G" (performing prime contracts with the government) and "B2B" (performing subcontracts with other companies).

Changes. Always require that changes to the contract be in writing and signed by both parties. The exception to this rule is the *Changes clause* from the Federal Acquisition Regulation (FAR). The *Changes clause* in the FAR is a notable distinction of government contracting, and the savvy prime contractor will *flow down* some version of the Changes clause to any subcontractor. Read more about the *Changes clause* in "Noteworthy FAR clauses" and "Negotiating Modifications and Change Orders." Also review the "Flow-Down Clauses" chapter. How you handle the process of changes will significantly influence your contract. Carefully review and negotiate any clauses or sections about changes.

Choice of law clauses address what state (or federal) laws will apply to the interpretation of the contract. If your contract devolves into litigation, remember that different states of America (such as Virginia or New York) have different bodies of law or *precedent* that apply to contractual interpretation. As strange as it may seem, the same contract can be interpreted very differently, depending on whether California or Louisiana state law applies.

Another complication arises if the contract is between two companies in two different states. Which state's laws apply? What if the contract is performed in a third state? To answer these questions before the contract is signed, companies include a choice of law section that explicitly adopts the laws of a specific state, for example, those of Maryland or Alaska.

Choice of venue. Venue refers to the physical location of the court system that your contract will use for any litigation. Choose the optimal venue because you may want to avoid expensive travel costs. Further, it may be difficult for you to find a good attorney in a faraway or foreign location. For these reasons, many contractors want a venue that is nearby, such as your company's state, region, or city. In sports, they call this the *home-field advantage*, where the local team is more comfortable playing at its hometown stadium. Negotiation of the venue clause revolves around who gets the *home-field advantage*.

Consider whether the *choice of law* and *choice of venue* clauses should align. Having a different choice of law from the choice of venue can significantly complicate any future litigation. For example, if your company is in New Jersey, do you really want to agree to use the law of Florida in the courts of California? Perhaps the simpler solution is to use the same state or location for both choice of law and choice of venue. However, there may be valid reasons for using a different state's laws. Consult your attorney for legal advice.

Classification (see security)

Clearance (see security)

Closeout clauses state the process and responsibilities to wind down the contract at completion. Closeout may include identifying outstanding invoices, returning property or documents, settling final payment, and providing written release of obligations. The government has its own process of closeout, but companies are largely free to negotiate their own closeout process or no closeout process at all. Just remember that the prime contractor's obligation to the government may require assistance from the subcontractor. For that reason, prime contractors may need to *flow down* certain closeout requirements to subcontractors.

Communications clauses designate whom to call, write, or email for various reasons. For example, "Contact John Doe, Facilities Clearance Officer, for any issues regarding security clearances" or "All invoicing and payment issues should be directed to the Accounting Department." Your company should have designated points of contact for issues like contracting, accounting, legal, and payments. Uniformly designate your points of contact in each of your contracts to streamline your operation. Take advantage of the specialized nature of your employees and officers.

Some clauses will limit or forbid communication with certain people or companies. For example, prime contractors may not want their subcontractors to speak or write directly to their government client.

Prime contractors want to limit or eliminate contact between the subcontractor and the government client. The prime contractor may fear that the subcontractor will spoil the client relationship or steal business away from the prime contractor. For these reasons, prime contractors often direct subcontractors to route all communication through the prime contractor. For example, "Subcontractor shall not contact the government client directly; all communication shall be directed to the prime contractor." As a subcontractor, you need to understand if and when you can communicate with anyone other than the prime contractor. For subcontractors that perform directly onsite with the government client, negotiating a reasonable and crystal-clear communications clause is critically important. Some subcontracts require close communication with the government client or some third party.

Confidentiality (see nondisclosure)

Conflicts of interest. Carefully review your obligations in the conflicts of interest clause. You may be required to notify someone or take special precautions if certain conflicts arise.

The classic case of a conflict of interest is for you to serve two masters. Your loyalty to one master conflicts with your loyalty to the other. For example, you sued another company over a government contracting dispute. Would you want to have the same attorney as the other company? In another example, you want to buy a house. Would you want your buyer's agent to be the same person as the agent representing the seller? In both cases, the attorney or real estate agent has a classic conflict of interest.

Another example of conflict of interest relates to government contracting. Let's say your company provides onsite support services for a federal agency. Your employees assist the government contracting officer in designing the *statement of work* and crafting the *request for proposals* for a multimillion-dollar contract for project XYZ. Your company has a classic conflict of interest if it wants to submit a proposal for project XYZ.

Since your employees helped to write the *statement of work* and *request for proposals*, you have insider information about project XYZ that your competitors do not have. Since your employees' government contract requires them to support the federal client, their dual loyalty to your company creates a conflict of interest between the federal client and their employer (your company). Your employees may write the *statement of work* or *request for proposals* in a way that favors your company. Your employees may leak—purposefully or accidentally—insider information that will give your company an unfair advantage in the competition. In this situation, your company has a classic *organizational conflict of interest* in competing for project XYZ.

Conflicts of interest are a constant concern because federal agencies spend taxpayer money on federal contracts, meaning agencies have a special duty to protect the interest of taxpayers. For this reason, the ethics rules for government contracting are stricter than for private-sector business deals. Government business must be conducted in a manner "above reproach," with "complete impartiality," and with "preferential treatment for none." The government's policy is to avoid any conflicts of interest or *even the appearance of a conflict of interest* in government-contractor relationships.

In turn, prime contractors need to deter their subcontractors from creating conflicts of interest, and must obligate their subcontractors to report any new conflicts.

Counterparts clauses provide the convenience of signing a contract in separate documents. Maybe you cannot travel thousands of miles to sign the original copy that your counterpart signed. Instead, the counterparts clause allows you to sign a different copy.

For example, company A signs one copy of the contract in Michigan. Company B signs a different copy of the contract in Hawaii. Due to the counterparts clause, there is no problem with this arrangement. The contract is valid despite being signed by two parties with two different copies of the contract.

Digital signatures, email, and online signature software largely eliminate the need for counterparts clauses that deal with "wet" or pen-and-ink signatures. Instead the parties can digitally sign or digitally transmit signed versions of the contract in a matter of minutes, with no need for extensive travel or colocation.

Definitions sections list several words, terms, phrases, or concepts with careful and thorough definitions. The goal is to have both contractual parties agree to the same definitions to prevent misunderstandings or conflicting interpretations. Spend some time on the definitions section. Define any terms of art, jargon, or even common words that could be misconstrued. Better to be safe than sorry!

The minimal effort to define important terms will prevent major problems during contractual performance. Many contract disputes could have been avoided if the parties had previously agreed to a single definition for a word or phrase.

Delivery clauses specify when, where, and how the products or services must be provided. For products, pay attention to who pays shipping cost, and who is liable for damage during shipping and before delivery. For services, you need to define the place of performance. In the 21st century, you may negotiate the option for telework or remote work rather than performing exclusively at the agency or company building. Be sure to negotiate maximum flexibility for remote work upfront, rather than petitioning for these conveniences during contract performance.

Disputes. Be careful with the disputes section because the word "disputes" is a *term of art* with a special definition in government contracting. The Federal Acquisition Regulation (FAR) has a specific clause that governs the disputes process (the *Disputes clause*). In contrast, nongovernmental contracts often address the disputes process in a variety of other ways. Distinguish whether the reference to disputes is a targeted reference to the FAR clause or a more general agreement about dispute resolution.

If your contract is a prime contract with the federal government, you cannot negotiate the Disputes clause. The contracting officer will include the standard version of the Disputes clause, which you must follow. The Disputes clause is a contractual implementation of a law originally called the Contract Disputes Act of 1978. That law established a formal process for submitting *claims* arising under or relating to government contracts.

First, the contractor submits a certified *claim* to the contracting officer, who must write a final decision. The contractor can appeal the final decision to the Court of Federal Claims or the boards of contract appeals. Next, the contractor can appeal to the Court of Appeals for the Federal Circuit. The final forum for appeal is the Supreme Court of the United States. If you need to submit a claim or request for equitable adjustment, I recommend you read my seminal article on this topic by emailing me at Christoph@ChristophLLC.com. I will provide you a free copy of the article and may assist you further.

Consider that prime contractors will want to *flow down* the process of the FAR-based Disputes clause. If the prime contractor is subject to the Disputes clause, the prime contractor may want the subcontractor to follow the same process.

If your contract is a subcontract or agreement between two companies, you can negotiate the contract language dealing with the disputes process. Some companies like to avoid formal litigation in courts by agreeing that all disputes will be handled first by arbitration. Arbitration is a form of *alternative dispute resolution* that is different from litigation in courts. Ask your attorney about the pros and cons of litigation versus arbitration.

Entire agreement (see integration)

Flow-downs. To learn about flow-down clauses, read the chapter, "Flow-Down Clauses."

Force majeure clauses provide an escape from the contract if there is some unforeseeable and cataclysmic event. *Force majeure* is a French phrase that translates to "greater force," implying the intervention of God. The phrase "acts of God" relates to these concepts. Events like war, natural disasters, and pandemics cannot be blamed on individuals but are instead "acts of God." Therefore, the contract parties agree that they are excused from performance if an event occurs as described in the force majeure clause. Consider the force majeure clause to be a form of risk insurance in the case of unpredictable and disastrous events.

Headings clauses explain that the titles or headings of individual sections are for the reader's convenience and do not limit, diminish, or affect the meaning of the contract. The headings clause eliminates the possibility of fouling up the entire contract because of poorly written or nonsensical headings (titles) within the contract.

Indemnity or indemnification clauses shift risk from one party to another. When you read *indemnify* you should think "agree to pay for the damages caused by someone." Indemnification clauses may require you to "pick up the tab" and pay for the mistakes or bad behavior of *other parties*. In this way, one party will *indemnify* — or agree to reimburse the costs of damages caused by — the other party.

Be careful with indemnity clauses because you could agree to suffer by "picking up the tab" for someone else's behavior, not just for your own actions. Some indemnity clauses require you to pay exclusively for damages caused partly by your mistakes, even if the other party in the contract is also at fault. While this arrangement is common, it does not mean it is optimal for your company or for every contract.

Consider what actions are covered by the indemnity, try to estimate the actual costs in case of failure or damages related to those actions, and negotiate to amend any arrangements that unfairly shift all the risk to your company no matter who else may be at fault.

Independent contractor relationship clauses specify that the parties to the contract will not create any other relationship such as partnership, employer-employee, joint venturers, agents, or the like. Instead, the parties agree that each company or individual remains separate and distinct as independent contractors. The reason so many contracts define the parties as independent contractors is that the other relationships (partnership, employer-employee, joint venturers, agents) increase risk by allowing one party to be liable for the other party's actions. For example, partners and joint venturers may be liable for the actions of the other partners or joint venturers.

Another consideration is that companies wish to avoid the possibility of a court interpreting an employer-employee relationship. Employers have special duties and responsibilities owed to employees, such as tax withholding and payment of such benefits as health insurance or paid leave. No company wants to be surprised with the cost of paying an "employee" who was supposed to be an "independent contractor." You can study famous examples of so-called "independent contractors" suing to obtain the benefits of employees by researching litigation regarding Microsoft in the 20th century and Uber in the 21st century. Both Microsoft and Uber faced significant lawsuits from so-called "independent contractors" who argued they were treated as employees and deserved to be classified and compensated as employees.

Most subcontracts involve two companies engaging in an *independent contractor relationship*. Most prime contracts between a company and the government define the prime contractor as an *independent contractor*. In fact, the term *independent contractor* is directly related to the broader term of *government contractor*. Distinguish between the employees of your company, who work in an *employer-employee relationship*, versus your subcontractors, who operate under an *independent contractor relationship*.

Inspection clauses should define who inspects, when they inspect, how they inspect, and what they inspect. Just like delivery and acceptance clauses, inspection clauses are dangerous because they can delay your payment. If your products or services fail the inspection process, your company may not get paid. Read more about delivery, inspection, and acceptance clauses in the chapter, "Noteworthy FAR Clauses."

Pay close attention the Federal Acquisition Regulation (FAR) clauses dealing with inspection. Multiple versions exist so you must read the full text of your inspection clause to understand your obligations. Generally, the inspection clause differs depending on whether you provide goods or services and whether your payment arrangement is fixed-price, cost-reimbursement, or time and materials.

Insurance clauses specify (1) what types of insurance coverage the parties must hold during contract performance, and also (2) the dollar limits of those policies. As a government contractor, your company probably needs several types of insurance. Even if your company has no government contracts and participates only in the private sector, your company probably needs insurance. Let's explore the different types:

General liability insurance protects against risks like bodily injury or property damage, which are physical, tangible risks. For example, general liability insurance may cover your company for litigation claims if your employee hurts someone else or destroys someone else's computer while performing work. General liability is important for any company, including government contractors.

Professional liability insurance protects against abstract risks like errors or omissions in the services your company provides. For example, professional liability insurance may cover your company for litigation claims if your employees provide inaccurate advice or commit negligence. Just like general liability insurance, professional liability insurance is important for any company providing professional services, including government contractors.

Workers' compensation insurance pays for medical expenses, lost wages, and rehabilitation costs to your employees who become injured or sick at work. Each state has its own, different workers' compensation requirements, but your company is required to pay these costs to employees who get hurt "in the course and scope" of their job. If you have no workers' compensation insurance, your company must pay these costs out-of-pocket. If you have insurance, the insurer pays these costs (in exchange for your monthly premiums). Many states require companies to carry workers' compensation insurance.

Integration clauses are designed to invalidate all other negotiated terms or conditions that are not written into the contract itself. Nothing discussed before the contract matters if it is not also written within the contract! *Integration, entire agreement, or merger* clauses are common in many different contracts. Your residential lease contract probably includes an integration clause.

The integration or *entire agreement* clause states that no promises, terms, conditions, or agreements are valid or enforceable unless they appear in writing in the signed contract. The purpose of the integration clause is to avoid disputes about preliminary discussions, conversations, or negotiations leading up to the contract. Instead, the integration clause states that all applicable agreements, terms, or conditions are *integrated* into the contract itself and nothing else is relevant — including prior discussions. You can save yourself plenty of trouble by including the integration clause in the contract. Another term for the *integration* clause or *entire agreement* clause is *merger* clause. The idea is that all agreements are *merged* within the contract itself, and that the contract itself is the complete and final agreement.

Intellectual property clauses are extremely important and one of the most complicated sections of any contract. If you want to become an expert in intellectual property contracting, my advice is to abandon your goal. Do not even try. Do not proceed by yourself. Quit. Then hire a competent attorney specializing in intellectual property *for government contractors*.

Do not hire an attorney who specializes in other areas of the law such as business litigation, family law, or white-collar crime. Do not hire an attorney who specializes in government contract law, but not specifically in intellectual property. You need to hire a specialized attorney, someone who focuses his attention on intellectual property *within federal government contract law.*

Intellectual property is vitally important to the survival of your company. Protect your intellectual property by investing in an excellent attorney who specializes in intellectual property within federal government contract law.

Invoices. For more information, read the chapter, "Getting Paid: Invoice and Payment Terms."

Joint and several liability are two distinct concepts that can be confusing. Let's simplify the two concepts. Under several liability, each party is liable only for itself. One party is not liable for the actions of the other party. In contrast, under joint liability, both parties are liable for the actions of the other party, in addition to being liable for its own actions. When you read *several liability*, think of the word "severed" as in "disconnected." You are liable only for yourself and therefore "disconnected" from the liability of others. When you read *joint liability*, think of how your joints "connect" your body parts. You are "connected" to the other party because you are liable for the actions of the other party, not just your own.

As you may imagine, liability is usually about who can be sued or who is on the hook to pay money for damages. Therefore, when you agree to *joint and several liability*, you give many options to someone who wants to sue you based on the contract.

Your adversary can sue you, individually, which falls under *several liability*. Your adversary can also sue you and the other party, together, which falls under *joint liability*. By giving your adversary more options to choose whom to sue, your adversary may look for who has the "deeper pockets."

By "deeper pockets," lawyers refer to the amount of money or how easy it is to take away that money in a lawsuit. Lawyers look for people and companies that have lots of money or money that is not protected from lawsuits. Therefore, under *joint and several liability*, your adversary may look at all the contractual parties and decide whom to sue.

Who has the most money? Whose money is least protected from lawsuits? Should we sue a single company alone and not bother with the others? Should we sue two of the three companies? Or should we sue every single company that is involved? Now you understand why joint and several liability can be so dangerous. Under joint and several liability, your adversary can sue you for the entire amount or spread those costs among all the parties. Even worse, even if you are not sued by the initiating party, whomever is sued can chase after you for the liability because you agreed to joint and several liability. Remember, at one time you agreed to these outcomes!

Key personnel clauses designate one or more positions as so integral to successful contract performance that special rules apply to their replacement. *Key personnel* have restrictions on if, when, and how they can be substituted with other people. The client will usually require advance notice and possibly written approval for the substitution of any key personnel.

Be careful when proposing or substituting key personnel because the replacement's qualifications, credentials, and performance will be heavily scrutinized. If your company wins a proposal using specific names for key personnel, the client will be livid if those specific people fail to show up on day one of the contract. Therefore, do your best to secure the future performance of your key personnel before using their resumes in your proposal. Keep your key personnel happy because they can make or break your contract.

Late payment clauses explain if and when late fees apply for late payments. For more information, read the chapter, "Getting Paid: Invoice and Payment Terms."

Limitation of liability clauses reduce to a specific dollar amount or completely eliminate certain types of liability. *Liability* refers to your responsibility to pay damages (money) for lawsuits or losses derived from the contract. The limitation of liability clause may completely eliminate an entire category of risk. For example, maybe the clause eliminates any liability regarding infringement of intellectual property. Or the clause may limit the liability to a specific dollar amount. For example, maybe the clause limits liability for breach of contract to no more than fifty million dollars.

Merger (see integration)

Nondisclosure clauses prevent you from sharing secret, nonpublic, confidential, or proprietary information—or maybe *trade secrets*—shared by your negotiation partner. Your contract may include a nondisclosure clause, but often you will sign a separate document devoted exclusively to this topic, commonly abbreviated as *NDA*.

Some companies require signature of a nondisclosure agreement before you enter into any negotiation or significant exchange of information, well before you review any contract to sign. Companies keep a firm grip on their secret, confidential, and proprietary information, so nondisclosure agreements appear early in the process.

Nondisclosure agreements can be one-way and *unilateral*, applied to just one contracting party. Or nondisclosure agreements can be two-way and *bilateral* or *mutually binding*, applied to both contracting parties. If you agree to protect your negotiation partner's sensitive information, it seems reasonable to ask them to return the favor. Therefore, if you encounter a one-way nondisclosure agreement, edit the clause to mutually protect both parties.

Nondisclosure agreements have several other names like *confidentiality agreement, proprietary information agreement,* and *secrecy agreement.* Part of the nondisclosure agreement may be a *non-disparagement agreement*, which forbids you from saying, writing, or communicating anything negative about the company or its leaders, employees, products, or services.

Noncompete clauses prevent your contracting party from directly competing with you in the future. For example, "The subcontractor agrees to not submit a proposal for or perform a federal contract with the Department of Education concerning financial audits for a period of one year after this subcontract expires."

To be enforceable, the noncompete clause must be within reason. For example, it may be difficult or impossible to enforce a noncompete clause that forbids your subcontractor from submitting a proposal for any government contract in the future. Such a noncompete clause may be considered unfair or unconscionable, therefore, invalid. The trick to writing an effective noncompete clause is to tailor the limitations to a specific industry, designated location or market, and relatively short time period. For example, trash collection (industry), Los Angeles (location), one year after contract expiration (time period). You need to ask your attorney about the laws of noncompete clauses in your specific jurisdiction. Find out what terms are enforceable for your industry.

Non-solicitation clauses prevent your contracting partner from stealing your employees or business partners, or from stealing your clients or potential customers. Finding, recruiting, hiring, training, and managing top talent takes time and money. Developing, proposing, winning, and performing contracts also takes time and money. You do not want your competitors or partners poaching your best people or most lucrative clients. For these reasons, you may want to include a *non-solicitation* clause that prevents the other party from hiring—or attempting to hire—your employees or business partners, and that forbids soliciting business from your clients or potential customers.

Non-solicitation clauses pose a similar challenge to *noncompete* clauses. If you write the non-solicitation clause too broadly, it could be challenged as unfair, unconscionable, and therefore invalid. The trick is to carefully tailor your non-solicitation clause to be reasonable and therefore enforceable. Ask your attorney about the laws of non-solicitation clauses in your specific jurisdiction.

Notice clauses define how the contracting parties accept responsibility for communication or messages about the contract. For example, the *notice* clause may require that relevant contract communication must be in writing and sent via certified mail with the US Postal Service. Or notice can be satisfied by email. You have discretion to decide what qualifies as giving the other party notice. The most convenient form of written notice is probably email. Consider whether you want notice to be satisfied when the communication is sent or whether you should require confirmation from the recipient. If you require confirmation to satisfy your written notices, the other party can ignore your communication to their advantage.

Notice clauses are especially important to define the process to trigger contractual events like option exercise, term renewal, modification, termination, or acceptance. You need to define what proper notice looks like, when it must be communicated, and to whom it should be sent.

Options. Read the chapter, "Negotiating Option Periods" to learn about options clauses.

Payment. Read the chapter, "Getting Paid: Invoice and Payment Terms."

Place of performance clauses specify where the services must be performed. In the 21st century, this section is where you should negotiate the right to telework or perform remotely, perhaps from your home.

Performance work statement (PWS). Read the chapter, "Negotiating the Statement of Work."

Period of performance clauses define the specific time interval(s) of the contract. Most government prime contracts for services have a total period of performance of 5 years, divided into five, 1-year periods of performance. The first year is called the *base year*. The second, third, fourth, and fifth years are called *option periods* or *option years* because the government decides whether or not to extend the contract. Learn more in the chapter, "Negotiating Option Periods."

Although the standard is 5 years, contracts and subcontracts can have any variation of periods of performance. For example, 6 months total, divided into a six, 1-month periods of performance. Another example is a 1-year base period followed by a 6-month option period. The variations are limitless. Be careful to limit the periods of performance, distinguish any option periods, and define the process to extend the contract. Any change to the period of performance should be in writing and signed by both parties.

Personnel (see key personnel)

Publicity or public releases. Some contracts include a *publicity* or *public releases* clause to limit or control the ability to announce any details of the contract. Companies may wish to keep secret the terms or existence of the contract. Or companies may fear their contract partner will release the wrong type of publicity. Many prime contractors want to completely control all public relations and announcements, so the subcontractor is contractually forbidden from any press releases or public announcements. A less extreme option is to require permission or written approval for one party to make announcements, so the other party can veto any problematic plans.

Scope of work. The *scope of work* section is usually a simple, short explanation of the purpose of the contract. While the *Statement of Work* is more detailed, the scope of work section paints in broad strokes the products to deliver or services to provide. Glancing at the scope of work section provides a basic understanding of the contractual purpose. Use this section to limit or preclude certain work that cannot or should not be performed under the contract. For example, the scope of work for a consulting contract may state that no legal advice or tax advice will be provided.

Security clauses may cover issues like the security clearance required by your employees or the classification level of the contract. A *security clearance* is granted by the US federal government to provide different levels of access to classified information or programs.

You may have heard of a *secret* or *top secret* clearance, which are just two levels of security clearance. To gain access to any information considered *secret*, you need a *security clearance* at the level of *secret* or higher, such as *top secret*. A security clearance granted to an individual person is called a *Personnel Security Clearance* or PCL.

A type of security clearance granted to a company is called a *Facility Security Clearance* or FCL. If your company is granted the FCL, it means your company is eligible for access to classified information. Therefore, similar to a PCL for an individual, your company's FCL will be limited to a certain level of classification such as *secret* or *top secret*.

Carefully review the *security* clause to ensure your company has the minimum level of FCL (Facility Security Clearance) and that your employees working on the contract hold the required PCL (Personnel Security Clearance). Just because your company has a *secret* FCL does not mean that each of your employees holds a *secret* PCL, nor is that a requirement. Distinguish between the *FCL for your company* and the *individual PCL of each employee.*

Severability clauses state that if any portion, section, paragraph, or statement in the contract is invalid or unenforceable, the remainder of the contract is, nevertheless, valid. For example, if the *noncompete* clause is later invalidated by a judge, the rest of the contract remains valid. Think of the *severability* clause as a way to preserve the contract if one or more individual sections turn out to be invalid.

Statement of work (SOW). Read the chapter, "Negotiating the Statement of Work."

Stop work. The government may insert a Federal Acquisition Regulation (FAR) clause that allows the contracting officer to abruptly stop all work on the prime contract. In turn, your subcontract may include some version of a *stop work* clause so the prime contractor can exercise this power when prompted by the government. As the subcontractor, require the prime contractor to provide proof of the government stop work order before exercising the clause against the subcontractor.

Termination. Read more about the *termination* clauses in the chapter, "Noteworthy FAR Clauses."

Travel clauses might define or limit how you can be reimbursed for travel costs. Let me tell you a secret. Many government contracts and subcontracts lazily limit companies to the Joint Travel Regulations or the Federal Travel Regulations. However, those regulations apply to the travel costs of federal employees, not company employees. While companies performing cost-reimbursement contracts may be limited to the rates specified in the Joint Travel Regulations or Federal Travel Regulations, that does not mean your company must follow the entirety of those regulations. In fact, your company has good reasons to make its own travel policy. Consider the difference between what your company *can bill on a specific contract* versus your *company travel policy*. Not all company travel will be related or billable to federal contracts. This distinction matters because your corporate policy can be more flexible, generous, and simple than the tedious rules for federal employees. Create a corporate policy and follow it, but do not be surprised by misinformed people who say, "Your company must follow the Federal Travel Regulations!" Examine your contract to know the rules.

Venue (see choice of venue and choice of law)

Waiver. When you *waive* your rights, you give up the ability to enforce them. You can waive your rights in writing, or you can waive your rights by action — or inaction! For example, by failing to require a late payment fee for 9 months in a row, you *waived* your right to enforce the late fees in the future. The next time the payment is late, you have lost (waived) your ability to require a late fee.

Waiver clauses in a contract define how a waiver happens or limit the ability to create waivers in specific circumstances. Some contractors do not want waivers to happen without express, written intent. To accomplish that goal for the *late payment fee* clause, the *waiver* clause would state that any waiver of rights under the *late payment fee* clause must be in writing, and that the failure to require late payment fees does not waive the right to collect them in the future. In this way, a *waiver* clause can protect your company from losing the future right to take some action or enforce some right that it forgot or chose not to enforce. In contrast, a *waiver* clause with the opposite goal may state that any failure to enforce that right is an effective *waiver* of that right in the future. Think carefully about whether and how you want to preserve your rights to enforce contract terms that you may not enforce every time. Also consider that in the absence of a *waiver* clause, your failure to enforce a contract term may be considered a *waiver* of your rights.

Wet signature. "Wet" signature refers to a handwritten, pen-and-ink signature by a person. The federal government and most companies will accept digital copies of signatures rather than "wet" signatures. Some companies are so old-fashioned — and some contracts are so important — that they require "wet" signatures, disallowing any other form of signature.

X-Men. If you read anything in your contract about the mutant superhero team known as the *X-Men*, please, be sure to email me at Christoph@ChristophLLC.com. I can help!

Thank you so much for reading my book. Make sure you read every book in *The Government Contracts in Plain English Series*: https://www.amazon.com/dp/B09MRCMWBD

Made in the USA
Columbia, SC
02 March 2022